# CHICAGO

|CONDENSED|

tom given

LONELY PLANET PUBLICATIONS
Melbourne • Oakland • London • Paris

# contents

Chicago Condensed
1st edition – September 2001

Published by
Lonely Planet Publications Pty Ltd
ABN 36 005 607 983
90 Maribyrnong St, Footscray, Vic 3011, Australia

Lonely Planet Offices
**Australia** Locked Bag 1, Footscray, Vic 3011
**USA** 150 Linden St, Oakland, CA 94607
**UK** 10a Spring Place, London NW5 3BH
**France** 1 rue du Dahomey, 75011 Paris

Photographs
Many of the images in this guide are available
for licensing from Lonely Planet Images.
(email: lpi@lonelyplanet.com.au)
Images also used with kind permission of the Art
Institute of Chicago and VAGA.

Front cover photographs
Top: Lake Michigan and the Chicago skyline
(Richard I'Anson)
Bottom: Downtown Citibank Building
(Richard Cummins)

ISBN 1 74059 068 6

Text & maps © Lonely Planet Publications
Pty Ltd 2001

Photos © photographers as indicated 2001

Printed by Colorcraft Ltd, Hong Kong

# how to use this book

## KEY TO SYMBOLS

✉ address

☎ telephone number

Ⓔ nearest El station

🚇 nearest train station

🚌 nearest bus route

🚗 auto route, parking details

🕐 opening hours

ⓘ tourist information

⑧ cost, entry charge

e email/web site address

♿ wheelchair access

⚕ child-friendly

✗ on-site or nearby eatery

V good vegetarian selection

## COLOR-CODING

Each chapter has a different color code which is reflected on the maps for quick reference (eg all Highlights are bright yellow on the maps).

## MAPS & GRID REFERENCES

The fold-out maps on the front and back covers are numbered from 1 to 7. All sights and venues in the text have map references which indicate where to find them; eg (2, C3) means Map 2, grid reference C3. All sights and significant venues are marked on the maps. For items not marked, the street is marked.

## PRICES

Price gradings (eg $10/5) usually indicate adult/concession entry charges to a venue. Concession prices can include senior, student, member or coupon discounts.

## WARNING & REQUEST

Things change – prices go up, schedules change, good places go bad and bad places improve or go bankrupt. So, if you find things better or worse, recently opened or long since closed, please tell us and help make the next edition even more accurate. Everyone who writes to us will find their name and possibly excerpts from their correspondence in one of our publications (let us know if you *don't* want your letter published or your name acknowledged). They will also receive the latest issue of *Planet Talk*, our quarterly printed newsletter, or *Comet*, our monthly email newsletter. Subscriptions to both newsletters are free. The very best contributions will be rewarded with a free guidebook.

Send all correspondence to the Lonely Planet office closest to you (p. 123).

**Lonely Planet** books provide independent advice. Lonely Planet does not accept advertising in guidebooks, nor payment in exchange for listing or endorsing any place or business. Lonely Planet writers do not accept discounts or payments in exchange for positive coverage of any sort.

# facts about chicago

Chicago is the great American city. New York is larger and Boston is older, but Chicago is the capital of the North American heartland.

It is called the Second City, the Windy City, The City That Works, City of The Big Shoulders. Chicago is all of that and more. A working city, first and foremost, where everyone has both feet planted firmly on the ground. People don't come for the scenery – there isn't any – and they certainly don't come for the weather. They come to do well and do good.

Where the prairie meets the lake they built a grand metropolis. Lakefront parks are lined with some of the best buildings of the 19th and 20th centuries, like the Rio beachfront, but with ice and snow. Downtown towers fill the sky, like the Manhattan skyline reworked by Louise Nevelson. In museums and galleries, paintings dazzle the eye. In clubs large and small, musicians arouse the ear. In dozens of theaters, actors engage the mind. And everywhere you go, people politely say 'please', and 'thank you' and 'after you.'

So take a chance on the weather. Let The City That Works work its magic on you.

*Chicago towers twinkle over the Midwestern plains.*

# HISTORY

The Potawatomi Indians who lived nearby called the marsh where you could portage from Lake Michigan to the Illinois River system 'Checaugou' after the wild onions and garlic there. In 1673, the Frenchmen Marquette and Joliet found a water link between Canada and Louisiana here.

Jean Baptiste Du Sable became the first known settler of any race in 1779. In 1803, the new US government built Fort Dearborn where the Michigan Ave Bridge now crosses the Chicago River. The Potawatomi wiped the fort out during the War of 1812. The government rebuilt in 1816, and the settlement was incorporated as Chicago in 1833, but Chicago was still a village until promoters began a canal between the river and the lake. When it finally opened in 1848, Chicago was a city of 20,000.

## 'Player with Railroads & the Nation's Freight Handler'

The first railroad arrived in 1850. By the beginning of the Civil War 11 years later, Chicago was the hub of a network connecting New York with the Midwest and West. Grain poured in, to be graded, sorted and shipped east. The Union Stockyards opened in 1865 and cattle poured in too, to be slaughtered and shipped out in new refrigerated boxcars. Factories sprung up producing building tools and machinery for new farms out on the prairies.

## Fire & Recovery

On October 8, 1871, a fire started on the southwest side of town. When it was over three days later, almost everything east of the river from Roosevelt Rd to Fullerton was gone, 300 people were dead and 90,000 people were homeless. The fire ignited a building boom that changed the nature of construction forever as property values pushed architects to develop steel-frame structures to rise high above overpriced land. By 1900 there were 1.7 million people in the city.

Richard Cummins

*Written in stone: friezes on the Michigan Ave Bridge tell the story of the city (see p. 40).*

Chicago celebrated its recovery with the 1893 Columbian Exposition. Daniel Burnham designed the fairgrounds in a Beaux Arts style imported from France. His City Beautiful concept integrating architecture and city planning swept across the country, leaving boulevards and Roman temples in its wake.

## The Great Migration

Despite race riots in 1919 and housing segregation that restricted blacks to a small slice of the South Side, 50,000 African Americans arrived in Chicago between 1910 and 1920 from the Old Confederacy, more than doubling the black population. Their numbers doubled again during the 1940s, making Chicago one of the blackest (and most segregated) cities in the North.

## The City That Works

After WWII, thousands of white city people headed to the suburbs, pulled out by freeways and cheap government loans and pushed out by fears of new black neighbors. In 1955, Richard J Daley became mayor and the head of the Irish-American political machine that ran the city.

*Big lake, big sky, big city*

Da Boss, as Daley was known, invested in roads, airports and transit systems while other big American cities decayed. However, his city did not work for everyone. The slums of Bronzeville were replaced with the largest housing projects in the country, leaving much of the South Side a no-go zone. Swaths of the West and North Sides were also replaced with vertical warehouses for the poorest in town. Daley ruled the city until his death in office in 1976, presiding over such low points as the riots after the murder of Martin Luther King Jr in April 1968 (when he issued his infamous 'shoot to kill' order) and the police riot during the Democratic National Convention that summer.

## Garden in the City

In 1982, Harold G Washington became Chicago's first African American mayor. He too died in office, after his first re-election in 1987, but left the city profoundly changed from the Richard J Daley years.

In 1989, Richard M Daley won his father's seat, which he holds to this day. He has worked to make the city an attractive place to live for people with choices by promising good parks and good schools. (He's still working on the schools, but has delivered on parks and landscaping.) Neighborhoods are coming alive and the city is blooming again. Population is up for the first time in 50 years (to 2.9 million in 2000). At this rate, the Chicago Cubs may win next year.

## ORIENTATION

Chicago sprawls along the southwest shore of Lake Michigan in the middle of the North American continent. Downtown, locally known as The Loop, sits on a square-mile peninsula where the Chicago River meets the lake. The city and its suburbs, Chicagoland as they say in the *Chicago Tribune*, fan out across the prairie in every direction, north into Wisconsin, east into Indiana and Michigan and west into the Illinois farm belt.

Aside from the lake and a few rivers and streams, there are no natural landmarks in the area. The line of skyscrapers along the lakefront is the key artificial landmark. The 'best' neighborhoods in the city and almost all the sights and attractions are in this strip.

The city is laid out in a grid, its streets are numbered 800 to the mile, starting from zero at State and Madison Sts. If you're at 3200 N Clark St, for example, you're four miles from The Loop and a half-mile from your dinner reservation in the 3600 block.

## ENVIRONMENT

Chicago's motto, *Urbs in Hortis* (City in the Garden), is more than a slogan. The original city charter declared that the lakefront would remain free and clear and clean for public use, and the businesspeople who built the city used their influence to keep it that way. Most city streets are lined with trees, free of trash cans and power lines, which are tucked away in the alleys. Inland neighborhoods are dotted with parks and playing fields that supplement the grand amenities of the lakefront areas.

*The Magnificent Mile: retail heaven*

Chicago draws its water from the lake, so the city fathers reversed the Chicago River to flow south into the Mississippi River system to keep lake waters clean.

The current Mayor Daley has spent millions on the local environment to keep middle-class people in the city. Since his first election in 1989, the city has planted 250,000 trees and installed countless acres of landscaping, from the wildflower garden in Grant Park to the baskets of flowers lining Michigan Ave.

## GOVERNMENT & POLITICS

For 100 years, the Democratic Party has run Chicago and surrounding Cook County. Most of that time, the Irish-American political machine based on the South Side has run the Democratic Party. When other big-city machines were dying in the 1950s, Richard J Daley's was still going strong.

When Daley died, however, a good deal of the machine's power died with him. African Americans, who now constitute about 36% of the population, took City Hall in 1983, but after Washington died in 1987, Richard M took City Hall back, with the backing of a much broader coalition than his late father had enjoyed.

The machine has proved a mixed blessing over the years. With its power to grease the wheels inside and outside of City Hall, The City That Works can often deliver better city services more efficiently than other big US cities. However, those people and neighborhoods without clout languish.

### Did You Know?
- One of every six jobs in the Chicago area is in manufacturing
- You can rent a decent one-bedroom apartment in a good neighborhood for about $1000 a month
- Over 30 million people visited in 1999 (1.75 million overseas travelers)
- Thirty-five Fortune 500 companies are headquartered in the area
- Chicago has 15 miles of beaches
- There are 77 Chicago neighborhoods
- Chicago has more Poles than any place outside Warsaw
- The city has over 200 parades a year

*Chicago's trading future is bright.*

## ECONOMY

Carl Sandburg's 1916 poem 'Chicago' is a hymn to the city's economy at the beginning of the last century:

> Hog Butcher for the World,
> Tool Maker, Stacker of Wheat,
> Player with Railroads and the Nation's Freight Handler,
> … City of the Big Shoulders.

Chicago is still City of the Big Shoulders, though the stockyards are closed and the airlines are eclipsing the railroads. Manufacturing is alive and well, as are warehousing and distribution. White-collar fields like real estate, finance and health care are thriving. The convention business is strong, despite competition from Las Vegas and Orlando, and the conventional tourist business is booming.

The city's success has trickled down to a large portion of its residents. In 1998, Chicago ranked first in the country on the buying-power index, second on total effective buying power and second on the number of households with effective buying power of $150,000 or more. All those dollars go farther in Chicago than they do on either coast.

# SOCIETY & CULTURE

Since it became a city in the 1860s, Chicago has been a federation of communities divided by class, race and religion. Nineteenth-century working conditions gave birth to a labor movement that by 1886 had 60,000 workers on the street demanding an eight-hour day. Catholics hailing from Ireland, Germany and Poland built churches and schools that formed the nuclei of ethnic villages in the exploding metropolis. The Germans and Irish also rioted to protest prohibition laws sponsored by Protestant lawmakers downstate, paving the way for the city's response to Prohibition.

Racism reared its ugly head with the migration of African Americans to Chicago in the first half of the 20th century. After WWII, 'block busting' by unscrupulous realtors fueled the flight of thousands of white Chicagoans to the suburbs. Those who remained lived in ethnic villages like Bridgeport (home of the Daleys) or the upper-middle class ghettos of apartments and row houses along the lakefront.

Chicagoans still tend to live in ethnic enclaves, but the characters of the enclaves have changed as new immigrants have arrived. Today, one in four people is Hispanic, and one in 10 Asian. Native-born immigrants, gay and lesbian young people and members of the professional classes of every race and orientation, are raising new questions about class as gentrification proceeds from the North to the South Side.

## Gangster Years

The exploits of gangsters during the Prohibition era of the 1920s left an enduring mark on Chicago. When the US went dry in 1920, Chicago went on drinking. With lots of money to be made smuggling in whisky from Canada and brewing beer at home, petty criminals went big time. Gangland killings made headlines, as when Dion O'Banion was shot in his flower shop across from Holy Name Cathedral on State St or when seven members of Bugsy Moran's gang were shot in a garage at 2122 N Clark St in the St Valentine Day's Massacre.

Al Capone went to prison in 1931, Prohibition was repealed in 1933, and African American gangs supplanted Italian-Americans by the 1970s, but the romance of the Roaring Twenties lives on.

## Etiquette

Maybe it's all that experience waiting for one another to pass through revolving doors, but Chicago is a 'please' and 'thank you' kind of place. Expect elementary manners in public.

Chicagoans are also easy-going about smoking. You'll find smoking sections in most restaurants (half the seats must be reserved for nonsmokers, but there aren't always the best seats in the house). Smoking is not allowed on El platforms because of the fire hazard.

Driving brings out some of the worst local behavior. Don't expect cars to stop if you are jaywalking across a neighborhood shopping street. Don't even think about trying it across Michigan Ave.

# ARTS

Chicago may be the Second City, but it is second to none in its civic commitment to the arts. Chicagoans believe in the value of culture for culture's sake. They are earnest about the arts, even if they may not like or even understand what they see or hear.

## Architecture

Chicago is to modern architecture what Florence is to the Renaissance. This is where people learned how to build beautiful buildings with iron and glass and steel – buildings by, of and for the industrial age.

Good Victorians that they were, the masters of the Chicago School conceived skyscrapers built of the new industrial materials, serviced with new machines like elevators

*The distinct architecture of the city is evident in its skyscrapers.*

and telephones, decorated with a style and grace inconceivable today. They set a standard and a tone that has survived to this day, as masterpieces of Beaux Arts, art deco, the International Style and postmodern styles attest from street corners around town.

## Literature

From Theodore Dreiser to James Farrell and Nelson Algren, writers since the turn of the 20th century have looked the City of the Big Shoulders right in the face without flinching and come up winners.

An extraordinary amount of their work is about the lives of the little people who make the big city go. Gwendolyn Brooks became the first African American to win a Pulitzer Prize, for her 1949 book of poetry *Annie Allen*, about day-to-day life in Bronzeville. Pulitzer Prize winner Studs Terkel has charmed readers with oral histories of the lives of ordinary people, while contemporary mystery writers Sara Paretsky and Scott Turow spin tales of the meaner streets of the city, its corruptions, its prejudices and its crimes. Even Nobel Prize winner Saul Bellow uses his hometown as a setting from time to time.

## Dance

Dance came late to Chicago, but the city is making up for lost time. The world-renowned Joffrey Ballet moved to town in 1995, joining established local groups such as the equally talented Hubbard Street Dance company. Modern dance and jazz dance are particularly popular.

## Theater

Forty years ago, Chicago theater was mainly about touring companies of shows from Broadway. Today *The Reader* lists 100 or more choices a week in the theater section, 10 or 20 of which are top-rate. From world-famous companies like Steppenwolf and the Goodman down to lesser-known outfits such as the Court, nonprofit companies set the agenda and tone of the theater scene. Directors and audiences take chances (ticket prices are reasonable), and actors and writers can hone their skills.

This farm club for the big leagues has produced actors like Gary Sinise, Joan Allen and John Malkovich and writers like David Mamet. It has also produced improv comedy as we know it today, honed at Second City and other companies by performers like Mike Nichols, Elaine May and Alan Arkin.

## Film

An amazing number of films have been shot in Chicago, from the *Blues Brothers* to *Risky Business* to almost anything by John Hughes. An even greater range of films is screened here, where museums, universities and local art houses present stuff that doesn't make it to the local megaplex. The rival film reviewers for the morning papers, Gene Siskel and Roger Ebert, became some of the best-known critics in the US before Siskel's death a few years ago. Ebert continues to engage film buffs with his column in the *Sun-Times* and his weekly national television show. The Gene Siskel Film Center at the Art Institute is moving into its own theater at State and Randolph Sts in the middle of the city's Loop Theater District.

## Music

After architecture, Chicago is probably best known for music. High culture is well represented by a world-class symphony and a nationally known opera company. Low culture is everywhere, from fancy jazz and funky blues clubs to rock and punk and world music sounds. Chicago took to new sounds in jazz and blues 80 or 90 years ago and continues to listen to new sounds today.

*Edward Hopper's* Nighthawks, *1942: see the real thing at Chicago's Art Institute (p.15).*

# highlights

Sightseeing in Chicago is a tour of what humans have created from a flat piece of land beside the flat waters of the Great Lakes. While there's little history or scenery, Chicago is renowned for its culture, with museums, universities and galleries galore; glorious buildings and parks from one side of town to the other; and cinemas, bookstores, jazz clubs and city streets bustling with life.

Come in winter and have the city to yourself. Come in summer and share it with others, so many others that at times you may wish for some snow. A nine-day **CityPass** (see p. 114) will save money and time in queues for six major attractions, and a CTA transit pass (see p. 110) will save time and money moving around town. Try hitting the biggest attractions (eg, the Sears Tower) first thing in the morning.

Whatever your interests, allow time just to wander the streets and parks and take in the mix of people and interests that makes Chicago Everyone's Kind of Town.

## Stopping Over?

**One Day** Spend the morning at the Art Institute, then head to Marshall Field's in The Loop for lunch. Window shop up Michigan Ave to the John Hancock Center. Take a look from the 94th-floor observatory, then dine on the Near North Side or the Gold Coast.

**Two Days** Breakfast at Lou Mitchell's, then take a Chicago Architectural Foundation tour. Lunch in The Loop or nearby at Wishbone, then visit Museum Campus. Dine on the North Side, then take in a play or a film.

**Three Days** Rent in-line skates or a bike and tour Lincoln Park, lunch there, or perhaps visit the Zoo. Explore Clark St (north of North Ave, 1600 north) and Broadway (up to Sheridan Rd, 3900 north). Follow dinner with a night at a blues or dance club.

### Chicago Lowlights

The weather and the distances are the lowlights of Chicago and there's not a lot you can do about either of them. Expect bitter cold and winds that can knock you off your feet in the winter, and heat waves and thunderstorms that can knock you out in the summer. Dress in layers like your mother taught you and you'll be fine. As for distances, you'll learn to endure long hikes or rides just as you endure the weather. At least you'll always know just how far you're going because of the 800-to-the-mile numbering system.

Our admittedly subjective, least favorite aspects of visiting Chicago include:

- Traffic in Lincoln Park and Lakeview on a Friday or Saturday night
- Trying to find parking on the street anywhere inside the city limits
- Waiting for buses in the evenings
- Malls along Michigan Ave (except when it's raining or snowing)
- Derelict parts of the Near South Side between Hyde Park and The Loop

# ADLER PLANETARIUM & ASTRONOMY MUSEUM (5, P10)

The Adler Planetarium would be worth a visit just for the view of the city from its front steps. Climb those steps, walk on in and find views of the universe that easily eclipse the sight of the Chicago skyline.

## INFORMATION

- ✉ 1300 S Lake Shore Dr, Grant Park
- ☎ 312-922-7827
- Ⓜ Roosevelt
- 🚆 Roosevelt
- 🚌 12, 127, 146
- ⊘ Mon-Fri 9am-5pm, Sat & Sun 9am-6pm (to 10pm 1st Fri every month)
- Ⓢ $5/4 (free Tues); CityPass
- ⓘ Unlimited shows, special lectures, telescope tours & demos, & tours on Far Out Fridays (5-10pm 1st Friday every month, $13/10)
- Ⓔ www.adlerplanetar ium.org
- ♿ good
- ✗ Galileo's

*Richard Cummins*

*Richard Cummins*

Start in the original building, the first planetarium in the Western Hemisphere. The original Zeiss projector continues to cast its images of the stars and other night-sky objects in the **Sky Theater**. After the show, investigate the size and structure of the universe in the **Gateway to the Universe Gallery** or poke through the world-famous collection of astronomical tools and special exhibits in the **History of Astronomy Gallery** downstairs.

Wander into the **Sky Pavilion** which surrounds the original building, take in the shows at the **StarRider Theater** or peruse the exhibits on the Milky Way, the solar system and the changing views of the cosmos over the past 1000 years. Drive a model of the Mars Rover over the Martian landscape or make a crater on the moon. If all these hi-tech shows and displays jangle your nerves, relax in the

Atwood Sphere, Chicago's oldest planetarium (dating to 1913), the only surviving walk-in planetarium in North America.

On the first Friday evening of the month if the skies are clear, Far Out Fridays features unlimited Sky Theater and StarRider shows, telescope viewing at the Doane Observatory, live lectures by Adler astronomers and other special demonstrations and activities.

*Everyone's an astronaut at Adler.*

**DON'T MISS**
- Pritzker Cosomology Gallery • Space Walk Gallery
- Milky Way Galaxy Gallery • view of The Loop from Galileo's

# ART INSTITUTE OF CHICAGO (5, L6)

The Art Institute may be the best single establishment in the city of Chicago. It's not just the collection, the best general collection of art in North America outside of New York or Washington. It's not just the art school, which has been part of the institute since the day it was opened. It's not just the Beaux Arts building that has been a landmark since the 1890s. It's the intersection of all of these things – how the Institute has become a fundamental institution in Chicago life.

The signs of that life are everywhere. Students fill the galleries, sketching and painting and discussing this work or that. Docent tours of school groups, seniors groups and informal groups of visitors run throughout the day. Continuing education programs run evenings and weekends exploring arts from painting to film to design.

Amid the activity hang the great impressionist and postimpressionist paintings that made the Art Institute's reputation, proof that the Chicago socialites who built the original collection had taste and style to match their money. Walk though Louis Sullivan's trading floor for the Chicago Board of Trade (salvaged when the original building was demolished) and see how the moguls enjoyed great art at work as they did at home. Sit in the Hilda Rothschild Gallery (home to Grant Wood's 1930 work *American Gothic*, at right, and Hopper's *Nighthawks*, see p. 12) or the Helen Birch Bartlett Gallery (home to *A Sunday on La Grand Jatte*) and see how that taste and style endure to the present day.

**INFORMATION**

- ✉ 111 S Michigan Ave, Grant Park
- ☎ 312-443-3600
- 🚇 Adams/Wabash, Monroe
- 🚆 Randolph
- 🚌 1, 3, 4, 14, 145, 147, 151
- ⏲ Mon, Wed-Fri 10.30am-4.30pm, Tues 10.30am-8pm, Sat & Sun 10am-5pm
- 💲 $8/5 (free Tues); CityPass
- ⓘ audio tours & guided tours, film series, lectures, children's programs
- 🄴 www.artic.edu
- ♿ excellent
- 🍴 Court Cafeteria

Richard Cummins

© The Art Institute of Chicago and VAGA

**DON'T MISS**

- Caillebotte's *Paris Rainy Day* • O'Keefe's *Black Cross, New Mexico* Ayala Altarpiece • Van Gogh's *Bedroom at Arles* • Warhol's *Mao 1973* • Monet's *Stacked Wheat*

# CHICAGO BOARD OF TRADE (5, M4)

The largest futures exchange on earth sits in a magnificent art deco office building at the south end of LaSalle St in the middle of The Loop. The building itself is worth a stop, 45 stories tall and topped with a statue of Ceres, the Roman goddess of grain and the harvest, one of the last local products of the Roaring Twenties.

Step inside and enter a world where fortunes have been made and lost every day for over 150 years. Traders in bright-colored jackets roam the hallways. Go up to the visitor center on the 5th floor and watch them in action from the galleries overlooking the two enormous trading floors as they shout bids and flash hand signals, buying and selling interests in everything from pork bellies to the Standard & Poors 500 index.

Although The Board started business trading interests in agricultural goods from Midwestern farms, in 1975 it expanded its reach to intangible financial products like money and securities. Today, business on the financial trading floor far outstrips the original agricultural trading business.

## INFORMATION

- ✉ 141 W Jackson Blvd, The Loop
- ☎ 312-435-3590
- Ⓜ Jackson, LaSalle
- 🚇 LaSalle
- 🚌 1, 7, 60, 126, 135, 136, 151, 156
- 🕐 Mon-Fri 8am-2pm
- 💲 free
- ⓘ educational presentation every 30mins Mon-Fri 9.15am-12.30pm. No children under 16
- ⓔ www.cbot.com
- ♿ good
- ✕ Ceres Coffee Shop

Richard Cummins

Liquid assets flow freely at CBOT.

## World Standards

Although Chicago did not invent the futures contract, Chicago traders created the futures market in the 1800s by standardizing grain and other commodity contracts, standardizing contracts for future deliveries of commodities, finally making the contracts freely transferable which converted the contracts into commodities themselves.

# CHICAGO CULTURAL CENTER (5, K6)

The Chicago Cultural Center is a Gilded Age palace of culture that has made a spectacular transition to new uses some hundred years later.

It was built between 1893 and 1897, in Burnham's Beaux Arts style to house the main branch of the Chicago Public Library. The city founders made no small plans here. Louis Comfort Tiffany designed the mosaics, glass dome and chandelier in the Preston Bradley Hall. He also modeled the main reading room (now the Sidney Yates Gallery) after the Doges Palace in Venice. Other artisans created an enormous stained glass rotunda dedicated to the Grand Army of the Republic (the Union Army in the recently concluded US Civil War) to let light into other reading rooms below.

Today, the library books are gone but the public still remains. A visitor's information center and a coffee bar occupy half of the ground floor. Upstairs, six different galleries feature exhibits of work by famous and not-so-famous artists from Chicago and points elsewhere. See anything from photography celebrating Chicago neighborhoods to conceptual art from contemporary Poland, all for free.

Richard I'Anson

## Museum of Broadcast Communications

The Museum of Broadcast Communications, which fills most of the first floor of the Center, tells the story of broadcasting with a focus on Chicagoland radio and television. See relics like the set from the Kennedy-Nixon debate in 1960, catch an old show or a legendary sports moment, or try your own hand at reading the news (you can take home a video if you can bear it).

Four performance spaces in the building offer music from children's choirs to opera or jazz. Were that not enough, the Center presents theater, dance, film and lectures throughout the year. Performances, whether noontime concerts or evening presentations, are also free.

# FIELD MUSEUM OF NATURAL HISTORY (5, P8)

The Field Museum is the largest and most important of the three institutions on Museum Campus on the south side of Grant Park. Founded by Marshall Field to house the anthropology and biology exhibits left over from the Columbian Exposition of 1893, the Field focuses on the related fields of anthropology, biology, geology and zoology. It's an odd assortment at first glance, mummies and masks and beetles and gemstones with **Sue**, the largest and most complete Tyrannosaurus rex skeleton in the world, looming over everything from the middle of the museum lobby.

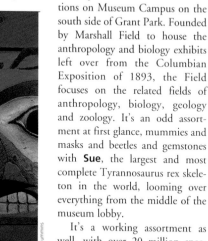

Richard Cummins

It's a working assortment as well, with over 20 million specimens in the collection, along with 250,000 books in the research library. Teams of scientists on view and behind the scenes use the specimens and the books to piece together the story of our world.

Standing guard at the Field Museum

Richard Cummins

While the Field Museum is famous for its anthropological work in New Guinea and other parts of the South Pacific, its Native American collection may be the best reason for a visit (with all apologies to Sue). The old-fashioned exhibits of Plains Indian clothing and artifacts are extraordinary and the new-fangled exhibits on the life of Native Americans from the Far North and Northwest are equally extensive. The centerpiece of the Native American section is a replica of a Pawnee sweat lodge, which puts dress and ceremonial objects into a context that few museums anywhere can match.

**DON'T MISS**
- McDonald's Fossil Preparation Labs • Maori Meeting House
- Chalmers' Topaz • Hall of Jade

# GRACELAND CEMETERY                    (4, A2)

Chicago was named for wild onions that grew in the marshes, and Chicago's first settlers were reminded of that fact when they began burying their dead in what is now Lincoln Park in the early 1800s. The Lincoln Park graves polluted the city's water and marred the city's views, so it was decided that Chicago needed a bigger graveyard on higher ground.

In 1860, 120 acres of land was acquired for this purpose, along with OC Simonds in 1861, who served as superintendent and chief landscape architect for the next 18 years. The resulting cemetery reflects the city built beyond it. Broad lanes wind through a parkland filled with flowers and bushes and trees. There's a little lake at the north end and you can hear the Red Line go by just past the east wall. In death as in life the great names of Chicago are clustered along the lakeshore – including Potter Palmer, Deering, William Goodman, Martin Ryerson and Wacker. Their tombs, like their houses, were designed by the great names of the day – Louis Sullivan, McKim White & Mead and Howard Van Doren Shaw the most prominent. Sullivan is buried nearby, as are thousands of less-celebrated residents of the 19th-century city.

Graceland today is more than a memorial to the men and women who built Chicago out of nothing. It has become an informal nature preserve, one of the safe stopovers for migrating birds on the Great Lakes Flyway.

## INFORMATION

- ✉ 4001 N Clark St, Wrigleyville
- ☎ 773-525-1105
- Ⓢ Sheridan
- 🚌 22
- ⏰ 8am-4.30pm
- $ free
- ⓘ maps (25¢) available at entry or from the guard
- ♿ excellent
- ✗ Deleece

*Great names of Chicago laid to rest*

**DON'T MISS**
- Getty Tomb • Mies van der Rohe grave
- Wunders Cemetery (across Irving Park Rd)
- Graceland Jewish Cemetery (south of Wunders Cemetery)

# GRANT PARK (5, K7)

Chicago's front yard is a Zen garden, more notable for its open and empty spaces than for the fixtures plunked down in it. This is no accident of history. The original grant of the shore to the city stated that the lakefront would remain 'forever open, free and clean.' Throughout the late 1800s and early 1900s department store magnate Montgomery Ward fought to keep it that way. Today, the line of 'Chicago-style' office buildings along the west side of Michigan Ave, facing the open park and the lake beyond, is one of the elemental images of Chicago.

There are a few urban facilities scattered about. The Illinois Central (IC) railroad tracks, which predate the park, run under the west side to the Randolph St station. The Art Institute straddles the IC tracks between Monroe St and Jackson Blvd, while the **Petrillo Music Shell** holds down the corner of Jackson Blvd and Columbus Dr. The rest of the space is open, filled with gardens and playing fields, decorated with statutes and fountains and relics of Chicago's past.

These open spaces come alive in spring and summer. **The Taste of Chicago** fills the park for two weeks (bring sunscreen and antacids). The Outdoor Film Festival presents movies during July and August. There's a blues festival, a jazz festival, a gospel festival and a country music festival, not to mention an Independence Day show featuring the '1812 Overture' and enough fireworks to burn down Chicago all over again.

## INFORMATION

- ✉ downtown lakeshore from Randolph St to Roosevelt Rd, The Loop
- ☎ 312-742-7529
- Ⓔ Adams/Wabash, Jackson
- 🚇 Randolph, Roosevelt, Van Buren
- 🚌 1, 3, 4, 14, 145, 147, 151
- ⏲ 7am-11pm
- Ⓢ free
- ⓘ tennis courts & skate rentals at Daley Plaza,
  ☎ 312-742-7648
- Ⓔ www.ci.chi.il.us
- ♿ excellent
- ✗ Artist's Snack Shop (412 S Michigan Ave; ☎ 312-939-7855)

Richard Cummins

Richard Cummins

*t's raining Zen...Hallelujah*

**DON'T MISS**
- Buckingham Fountain • Rose Garden
- Wildflower Works • Venetian Night at Monroe St Harbor

# JOHN HANCOCK CENTER (5, E6)

The John Hancock Center is the best modern building in Chicago *not* designed by Mies van der Rohe. This city-in-the-sky is beautiful, practical and offers visitors and residents the best view even though the rival Sears Tower is hundreds of feet taller.

Its beauty lies in its proportions. Massive columns soar from its base, a clean connection between tower and ground. The cross braces highlight the structure and emphasize the tension between the glass walls and their steel supports.

Its practicality lies in its design. The pyramid accommodates commerce at the base, offices in the middle, apartments above and a skydeck and restaurant at the top, each use needing progressively smaller and smaller floors to function efficiently. Even the cross-bracing is practical, reducing the amount of steel needed to build the building while assuring that it can withstand winds of over 120 miles an hour.

**INFORMATION**

- ✉ 875 N Michigan Ave, Gold Coast
- ☎ 312-751-3681
- ⊖ Chicago
- 🚌 3, 10, 125, 145, 146, 147, 151
- ⏰ 9am–midnight
- 💲 $7/5
- ⓘ self-guided audio tour $3 ($4 for 2); interactive displays highlight 80 local attractions below
- ♿ excellent
- ✗ L'Apetito

Its view stems from its location. A mile north of The Loop and just south of the Oak Street Beach, the Hancock presents a panorama of the center city from the Water Tower to the Sears Tower and a straight shot up the lakefront, past the convergence of Michigan Avenue and Lake Shore Drive north to Lincoln Park, the North Side neighborhoods and the North Shore suburbs beyond. All this without the lines and the videos one must endure to see the city from the Sears Tower.

*Late-afternoon shadows of buildings across Lake Michigan*

**DON'T MISS** • Pressing your nose against the glass after a martini in the Signature Room • The North Shore waterfront on a clear cold day

# LINCOLN PARK (4, E4)

Lincoln Park is the crown jewel of the Chicago Park District, such a key component of the city that one can no more imagine Chicago without Lincoln Park than one can imagine Paris without the Champs Élysées.

## INFORMATION

✉ North Lakeshore from Oak St to Hollywood Ave, North Side

☎ 312-742-7726

🚇 CTA Red Line stations from Clark/Division north to Bryn Mawr

🚌 135, 136, 145, 146, 147, 151

🕐 7am-11pm

💲 free

ℯ www.ci.chi.il.us

♿ excellent

✗ Café Brauer (near South Pond)

Tom Given

It's a huge piece of land – 1200 acres stretching about six miles from the Oak St Beach in the south to Hollywood Ave in the north. It's the front yard of the ritziest neighborhoods in town and a playground for hundreds of thousands of Chicagoans who live in more modest districts to the west.

If you can't find something to do here, you're simply not trying. Athletes can enjoy miles of bike paths, two sets of tennis courts, a driving range and a nine-hole golf course among other things. Sailors can dock at one of three harbors (the Diversey Harbor, set on the inside of Lake Shore Dr is reserved for power boats, Belmont Harbor and Montrose Harbor on the outside of the Drive are home to sailboats that can't get under the bridges). Landlubbers can rent a paddleboat on the South Pond or just enjoy the city views.

Miles of paths crisscross the park, perfect for cross-country skiing in the winter and running, walking and in-line skating almost year-round. Miles of beaches line the waterfront, perfect for swimming and sunbathing (the water is usually clean and cold). The North Avenue Beach House and Foster Avenue Beach House provide changing rooms, restrooms and snack bars in season. The Chess Pavilion near the North Ave beach shelters players who come from all over the city, chess clocks in hand, for serious competition or spectating.

The **Zoo** in the south end of the park is the center of the action. It's

*Run, ski, walk ... or just sit and relax in Lincoln Park.*

Richard Cummins

*Enjoy the serene landscape with a leisurely stroll.*

open daily 9am to 5pm, and it's free, so you can wander in and out through the pavilions and animal houses on your way to somewhere else. There are over 1600 animals here, residing gracefully on 35 acres in the shadows of the apartment buildings lining Lincoln Park West. The Zoo has two separate primate facilities, a flamingo house, a penguin house, and a sea lion pool with free shows at feeding times. Perhaps the best single pavilion is the **McCormick Bird House** where birds live in re-creations of their natural habitats, sheltered from Chicago's skies. It's no wonder that the Zoo is the second-biggest drawcard in the city, after Navy Pier.

Just north of the Zoo sits the **Lincoln Park Conservatory**, three acres of gardens under glass. It's also open daily 9am to 5pm, and also free. Filled with palms and orchids and other plants from warmer climes, it is a great spot to warm up on a cold winter day. Enjoy the permanent plantings, and special shows held throughout the year, such as the azalea show in late February and early March that heralds the approach of spring. Just north

of the Conservatory, the **Peggy Notebaert Nature Museum**, opened in 1999, has a butterfly haven, a city science exhibit and other temporary exhibits indoors (open Mon-Fri 9am-4.30pm, Sat & Sun 10am-5pm, admission $6/4/3). There's also an outdoor pond and walkway that you can enjoy any time for free.

Tom Gwen

*Time for a change: North Ave Beach House*

**DON'T MISS** • Elks Veterans' Memorial (Lakeview Ave at Diversey Pkwy) • Totem Pole (Lake Shore Dr at Addison St) • Farm in the Zoo (Cannon Dr at Armitage Ave) • Standing Lincoln (LaSalle Dr at N Stockton Dr)

# MUSEUM OF SCIENCE & INDUSTRY    (7, D7)

The Museum of Science & Industry is the original American techno-museum, a permanent science fair that delights children and adults alike.

Richard Cummins

The MSI sits in the Palace of Fine Arts, the last great surviving relic of the 1893 Columbian Exposition. It was conceived by Julius Rosenwald, chairman of Sears Roebuck, after a trip to the Deutsche Museum in Munich in 1911, and opened as part of the Century of Progress Exposition in 1933. It was one of the first museums both to enlist businesses to create exhibits and programs and to present interactive exhibits to the public.

Today, the MSI houses 800 different exhibits in 350,000 sq ft of exhibit space. Its most famous exhibit, the working coal mine, has run from opening day in 1933. As science and industry progress, the MSI adapts its shows. Visitors can see a Boeing 727 and space capsules (Aurora 8, Apollo 7) as well as antique cars and locomotives. New exhibits focus on AIDS and HIV, brain and computer imaging and the Internet. The five-story Omnimax theater presents two films every day.

Long-time favorites include a German U-Boat, captured off the coast of Africa in 1944 and shipped to Chicago in 1954 and the Silver Streak, a streamlined passenger train built for the Burlington Northern in the 1930s. Be prepared for some long lines for the most popular attractions during the weekends and school holidays.

These toys are just as entertaining for the big kids.

# NAVY PIER (5, G10)

Navy Pier is an urban playground that works. Built as a shipping terminal and public entertainment space in 1914, converted into a US Navy training facility in 1917 and again in 1942, this mile-long pier contains a museum, restaurants, shops, theaters, exhibition spaces and acres of parking.

The literal and metaphoric highlight of the Pier is the 15-story **Ferris Wheel**, which presents unparalleled views of the city from out in the middle of Lake Michigan. Below the Ferris Wheel sits a reflecting pool that converts into an ice rink in winter and the **Crystal Gardens**, a one acre garden filled with palm trees housed in a six-story greenhouse.

The **Chicago Shakespeare Theater** is located halfway down the Pier. The 550-seat theater is modeled after the Swan Theater in Stratford-on-Avon, a graceful combination of Elizabethan form and modern comforts.

Many of the best attractions at the Pier are seasonal. A half-dozen different boat rides depart from the docks on the south side of the Pier depending on the weather. **The Skyline Stage** next to the Ferris Wheel presents a wide range of different shows from Memorial Day to Labor Day. Other attractions,

## INFORMATION

- ✉ 600 E Grand Ave at Lake Shore Dr, Near North
- ☎ 312-595-7437
- 🚌 124 express; 29, 56, 65, 66; 120 & 121 rush hrs only, free trolley from Grand St El station & cnr of State & Rush Sts
- ⏱ May-Aug Sun-Thurs 10am-10pm, Fri & Sat 10am-midnight (weather permitting); Sept & Oct Mon-Thurs 10am-9pm, Fri & Sat 10am-11pm, Sun 10am-8pm; Nov-Apr Mon-Thurs 10am-8pm, Fri & Sat 10am-10pm, Sun 10am-7pm
- 💲 free; admission charges apply to most attractions
- ⓘ Ferris wheel open 11am-6pm (weather permitting)
- 🅴 www.navypier.com
- ♿ excellent
- 🍴 Food Court in Family Pavilion

such as the IMAX theater that shows special features and Hollywood films, the Navy Pier Players and the Children's Museum, are open year-round.

**DON'T MISS**
- Smith Stained-Glass Museum • WBEZ (FM 91.5) studios
- View of the city from the beer garden

# SEARS TOWER (5, L3)

At 1,454ft (about 440m) the Sears Tower was the tallest building in the world when it was built and it is still the tallest building in the world today under two of four accepted international standards. It has the tallest occupied floor and the tallest roof. The structural tops of the Petronas Towers in Kuala Lumpur are 19ft (9m) taller than the structural top of the Sears Tower and the antennas on the World Trade Center in New York top both Petronas and Sears.

## INFORMATION

- ✉ 233 S Wacker Dr, The Loop
- ☎ 312-875-9696
- ⊕ Quincy, Jackson
- ▣ Northwestern, LaSalle
- ▣ 1, 7, 60, 126, 135, 136
- ⊘ 9am-11pm
- ⑤ $9.50/7.75/6.75; CityPass
- ⓘ buy tickets in advance to skip one of the queues
- ⒠ www.sears-tower.com
- ⚒ good
- ✗ Mrs Levy's Delicatessen (restaurant level downstairs; see p 79)

By any standards, it's gigantic. One hundred ten stories with 4.5 million gross feet of space, ground floor lobbies three stories tall and two sky lobbies mid-tower.

Like its cousin the Hancock Center, the Sears Tower is an exercise in engineering. Instead of cross-bracing a single column, the Sears Tower engineers designed a set of nine identical columns that they tied together for a reasonably light weight frame. Look for them on the exterior.

The crowds visiting can be as gigantic as the Sears Tower itself. Over 1.5 million people visit the Skydeck every year and there will be times in the summer when you think every single one of them is in front of you in the lines.

When you finally do make it, all Chicagoland is at your feet. To the north and east, there's a thicket of skyscrapers and the lake. To the west and south, the city and the suburbs sprawl out across the prairie.

Richard I'Anson

Richard Cummins

*Searing height*

**DON'T MISS**
- The far shore of Lake Michigan on a clear day
- Calder sculpture in west lobby • City lights at dusk

# JOHN G SHEDD AQUARIUM (5, P8)

The Shedd Aquarium looks like the little sister to the Field Museum next door at the Museum Campus on the lakefront. Comparisons can be deceiving. In its old Greek temple building and new glassed-in addition that rings the lakeside of the original building, the Shedd houses one of the largest collections of water fauna in the entire world.

The original building is lovely outside but sadly dated inside, with one large **Caribbean Reef** tank in the center of the structure and small tanks lining the walls of the wings that run off from the center like the spokes of a wheel. The fish are there, up close and personal, but they do look a little cramped in their accommodations.

Things change down the stairs in the new **Oceanarium**. You'll find an enormous set of open pools, landscaped with rocks and evergreens to look like an inlet somewhere in the Pacific Northwest. There are sea otters and harbor seals, a set of Pacific dolphins and five beluga whales from Canada's Hudson Bay. The dolphins put on

a show several times a day, a little SeaWorld action in an otherwise fairly serious setting. If you don't care to watch dolphins do tricks for fish and applause, try one of the series of talks on offer about otter, penguin or beluga whale habitats, check out the special exhibits on the mezzanine level of the Oceanarium, or go back to the main building to watch divers feed the fish in the Caribbean Reef.

## INFORMATION

- ✉ 1200 S Lake Shore Dr, Grant Park
- ☎ 312-929-2438
- Ⓞ Roosevelt
- ⓡ Roosevelt
- 🚌 12, 146
- ⏲ winter weekends, holidays & summer 9am-6pm; winter Mon-Fri 9am-5pm
- ⓢ $15/11, some attractions extra; basic admission free Mon & Tues Sept-Feb
- ⓘ free tours on different topics daily at 2.15pm winter; 9.45am & 4.15pm weekends, holidays & summer (sign up at information booth in main lobby)
- ⓔ www.sheddnet.org
- ♿ good
- ✕ Bubblenet Food Court

Richard l'Anson

There's something fishy about this shed.

**DON'T MISS**
- underwater views of dolphin and whale ponds • Penguin Pool
- Amazon Rising exhibit • Illinois Rivers and Lakes exhibit

# HAROLD G WASHINGTON LIBRARY (5, M5)

Harold G Washington, the only African American mayor of Chicago, was a larger-than-life figure. The Harold G Washington Library – central branch of the Chicago Public Library and the largest public library in the world – is a fitting tribute to a man who used books and learning to smash barriers throughout his life.

Like so many Chicago institutions, the library tells its story with basic statistics. It sits nine stories tall and covers a full city block. It has 756,000 sq ft of space, holding over 1.9 million books and millions of other documents on over 70 miles of shelving. There's room for over 2300 readers and seats for hundreds more in its auditorium and meeting rooms.

The building is not one of the great structures of the city, although it does have its charms. A neoclassic design in granite and red brick, it sits gracefully amid the old department stores that line this part of State St. The top floor holds the Winter Garden and a sunny little cafe with views to the south.

You'll find all the mod cons you'd expect from the world's largest public library and more. Use the computers on the 5th floor to check your emails, surf the Internet or use basic programs like MS Word. You'll also find reference materials in English and other languages, newspapers from home (wherever home happens to be) and magazines in languages from Albanian and Catalan to Vietnamese and Yiddish. Free programs, lectures and art exhibits for adults and children round out the offerings.

## INFORMATION

- ✉ 400 S State St, The Loop
- ☎ 312-747-4136
- Ⓔ Library, Jackson
- Ⓡ LaSalle, Van Buren
- 🚌 1, 22, 29, 62, 145, 146, 147, 151
- ⏲ Mon-Thurs 9am-7pm, Fri & Sat 9am-5pm, Sun 1-5pm
- $ free
- ⓘ monthly calendar of events & tour information available at information desk on 1st floor
- Ⓔ www.chipublib.org
- ♿ good
- ✕ Beyond Words Café (Mon-Sat 11am-3pm)

Tom Given

## Harold G Washington

Chicago may have been founded by an African-American fur trader, but it took almost 200 years for another African-American to become mayor of the city. Born at Cook County Hospital in 1922, Harold Washington graduated from Northwestern University law school in 1952 after serving in WWII.

First elected to office in 1965, he became mayor in 1982 when then-mayor Jane Byrne and current mayor Richard M Daley split the white vote in two. He beat Richard M. in a one-on-one in 1986 but died at his desk of a heart attack in 1987.

# WRIGLEY FIELD                     (4, B2)

The 'Friendly Confines' of Wrigley Field is the most perfect space in the world of baseball. Fenway Park in Boston is a close runner-up, but against Wrigley it looks like a set of spare parts.

Wrigley looks and feels like it grew naturally out of the ivy that covers its red-brick outfield walls. The stadium was built in 1914; the scoreboard, bleachers and ivy were added in 1937. The primary intrusion of the post-war world is the set of lights that brought night baseball to the North Side in 1988. There is a set of private boxes on the mezzanine and there's even an elevator on the third base concourse, but Wrigley today retains the look and feel of ballparks from the newsreels.

The sense of history and order is so strong one could say that Cubs fans are more attached to their park than they are to their team. The infamous record of the Cubs does have something to do with this anomaly. Unlike the Boston Red Sox, the Cubs rarely even rate as contenders. They last won the World Series in 1908 (the Sox won in 1918, the year before they traded Babe Ruth to the Yankees) and last appeared in a World Series in 1945. Still, when the sun is shining in the bleachers and the crowd is singing during the seventh inning stretch, there's no better place in Chicago to be.

**INFORMATION**

- ✉ 1060 W Addison St, Wrigleyville
- ☎ 773-404-2827
- Ⓔ Addison
- 🚌 8, 22, 36, 152
- ⏱ park opens 2 hours before game time
- ⓘ tours available 6-10 times each season; $15 ☎ 773-404-2827 for details and reservations
- e www.cubs.com
- ♿ limited/good
- ✗ Cubby Bear Lounge (1059 Addison St; ☎ 773-327-1662)

## Those Ivy Covered Walls

In 1937, Cubs manager Bill Veeck planted ivy along the edge of the new outfield wall. Over 60 years later, the ivy is the hallmark of Wrigley Field and the secondary symbol of the Cubs. Countless fans have stolen cuttings over the years. Others have even scattered ashes of loved ones down the outfield wall, despite firm management policies against such memorials.

*History looms large at Wrigley Field.*

# FRANK LLOYD WRIGHT HOME & STUDIO (3, D4)

Frank Lloyd Wright came to Oak Park as a promising young man in the late 1880s and left it as a well-known middle-aged man 20 years later. In

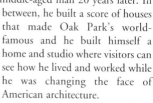

Raymond Hillstrom

between, he built a score of houses that made Oak Park's world-famous and he built himself a home and studio where visitors can see how he lived and worked while he was changing the face of American architecture.

Tours start in the home, built shortly after he arrived. The exterior, with its leaded glass and shingled siding, anticipates the move from the Victorian to the modern. The decorated interior shows Wright's debt to his mentor Louis Sullivan. The open plan of the ground floor, each room flowing into the others, was Wright's own revolutionary idea.

Both house and studio have built-in cabinets and furnishings that complement the overall design. The dining room, with soft indirect lighting from behind a stained-glass screen, a warm brick-tiled hearth and a wide window ledge in lieu of a sideboard or china cupboard, demonstrates how Wright designed spaces for people, not objects.

The spaces in the studio show Wright in top form. The 2nd-floor drafting room is a hexagon suspended above a square base, covered with patterns of light from the stained-glass skylight. His private library is an octagon with poured concrete floors lit by clerestory windows and lined with cabinets and cork boards on screens.

*Read and Wright: Frank's private library.*

# UNIVERSITY OF CHICAGO          (7, D4)

John D Rockefeller called the University of Chicago the best investment he ever made. He never made a dime on it, not that he needed any more dimes when he founded it in 1891, but he derived great satisfaction from creating one of the great universities of the Western world.

UC has been on the cutting-edge of academia since it opened as a coeducational, nondenominational school at a time when private schools were usually church-related and almost always men- or women-only. It pioneered the four-quarter academic year and adult education courses. It created the new academic field of Law & Economics and served as incubator for the 'Chicago Schools' of economics, sociology and literary criticism. More than 70 Nobel laureates have worked here in some capacity, six currently on duty. Enrico Fermi and Co first split the atom here, under the stands of Stagg Stadium on December 2, 1942.

All this takes place amid faux-Gothic splendor sprawling over a quiet corner of Hyde Park in the city's South Side. Rockefeller apparently believed exceptional people deserved exceptional environs and he went all-out to fund a vision of an English college complete with gates, chapels and towers. Take a walk through the main quadrangle and into the **Bond Chapel** and see for yourself just how well he succeeded. Then visit some of the university museums and galleries and performance spaces and see, too, how Rockefeller's legacy has survived the past 100-plus years.

## INFORMATION

✉ 1st fl, Ida Noyes Hall, 1212 E 59th St, Hyde Park
☎ 773-702-9739
🚇 55th St, 57th St, 59th St
🚌 4
🕐 Visitor Center Mon-Fri 10am-7pm
$ free
ⓘ free 1hr campus tours Mon-Fri except major holidays Dec-Feb 10.30am, Mar-Nov 10.30am & 1.30pm; mid-Sept to mid-Nov Sat 9.30am & 11.30am
e www.uchicago.edu
♿ excellent
✗ Hutchinson Commons (north end of main quad)

*Great environs for great minds.*

• Bond Chapel • Rockefeller Memorial Chapel • Oriental Institute • Court Theater

# sights & activities

Chicago's sights and activities are clustered along the lakefront and in a few inland districts near The Loop and the Near North Side. Most major attractions are within a mile of the lake and within a half-mile of the Red Line or the Michigan Ave bus lines.

Many of the great buildings and great museums are in **The Loop** or nearby in **Grant Park**. You'll find the great stores and grand hotels over the Michigan Ave Bridge on the **Near North Side** between the river and Oak St. The warehouse district to the west, **River North**, is filled with galleries, shops and clubs.

The **Gold Coast**, from Oak St to North Ave, is the toniest residential area in town, a sharp contrast to the **Cabrini Green** projects just west of Orleans (a no-go zone for visitors). North and west are **Old Town** and **Lincoln Park**, home to college students, straight 20-somethings and well-to-do families that came back to town or never left.

**Lakeview** and **Wrigleyville** beyond are the most interesting neighborhoods in town, a mix of gay and straight residents with wonderful shopping, eating, and entertainment. **Uptown** to the north has a thriving Vietnamese community, while **Andersonville** along Clark St west of Uptown, remains Swedish in places.

Outside the North Side are **Wicker Park** on the Near Northwest Side and **Hyde Park** on the South Side, the most bohemian districts in town. Wicker Park is known for artists and music, Hyde Park for intellectuals and books.

---

### Rest for the Weary

The large number of quasi-public spaces in Chicago means a better restroom situation for the traveler than in most US cities. You'll find good facilities in the vertical **malls along Michigan Ave**, which are generally open Mon-Sat 10am to 7pm (noon to 6pm Sunday) and in the large hotels in The Loop and the Near North Side. The restrooms at the visitor information centers at the **Chicago Cultural Center** and the **Water Tower** are also open during business hours (generally Mon-Sat 10am-7pm, Sun noon-5pm). If you're stuck on the west side of The Loop, duck into the **Thompson Center** (Mon-Fri 9am-5pm) or head over to the **Northwestern Station**, open seven days a week.

---

### Far From the Madding Crowd

Everyone needs a little quiet time sometimes. In good weather, head to **Grant Park**, **Lincoln Park** (at right) or one of the neighborhood spots like **Washington Square** on the Near North Side or **Oz Park** near DePaul University. In bad weather, quiet spaces are harder to come by. The Winter Garden on the top floor of the **Harold G Washington Library** is quiet, as is the rest of the library. Some of our other favorites are the food court on the 7th floor of Marshall Field's downtown and the coffee bars along Clark St and Broadway from Fullerton north to Addison.

# NOTABLE BUILDINGS

### 860-880 N Lake Shore Dr (5, E7)

This pair of apartment towers by Mies van der Rohe are on everyone's short list of the best buildings in Chicago. Examine their exteriors closely from the street and see why. The proportions are perfect, the finishes first-rate, the lobbies as elegant as his pavilion in Barcelona that gave the world Barcelona chairs.
✉ 860-880 N Lake Shore Dr, Near North 🚌 145, 146, 147, 151, 157 ⏲ private

### Auditorium Building

(5, M6) Adler and Sullivan would be famous today even if the Auditorium were the only building they built. The facade of this 10-story hotel and office building is a joy, with its heavy granite walls and gentle ornamentation. The 4000-seat auditorium inside may be the best and most beautiful theater in the US.
✉ 430 S Michigan Ave, The Loop ☎ 312-431-2354 Ⓣ Library, Harrison 🚌 6, 22, 36, 151 ⏲ vary, call ahead ⑤ $5/4 ♿ good

### Carson, Pirie, Scott Building (5, K5)

The Carson, Pirie, Scott Building shows how Louis Sullivan could marry the clean lines of a steel-frame office building with his trademark decorative motifs. Get close and personal with the cast-iron filigree work around the ground floor and the main State St entrance.
✉ 1 S State St, The Loop ☎ 312-641-7000 Ⓣ Washington 🚇 Randolph

🚌 6, 29, 36, 62, 146 ⏲ Mon-Wed 9.45am-7pm, Thurs 9.45am-8pm, Fri 9.45am-7pm, Sat 9.45am-6pm, Sun 11am-6pm ⑤ free ♿ good

### John J Glessner House

(6, C5) This Gilded Age mansion was designed in 1887 by Henry Hobson Richardson, before the social set moved north to the Gold Coast, filled with

## Chicago Styles

Chicago Architecture starts with the *Chicago Style* in the late 19th century, as Sullivan & Adler and others designed commercial buildings with clean lines and lots of windows, first of brick and stone and later of steel and glass (Hotel Burnham, p. 102). The formal and fussy *Beaux Arts* style imported from France arrived in 1893 (Chicago Cultural Center, p. 17) and held sway until *Art Deco* appeared during the 1920s (Chicago Board of Trade, p. 16). The industrial *International Style* arrived with van der Rohe in 1940 (860-880 Lake Shore Dr, p.33), setting the tone until *Post Modernists* like Jahn returned to traditional forms as at the United Terminal at O'Hare.

Tom Given

## The Burnham Plan

After the great success of the 1893 Columbian Exposition, Daniel Burnham was hired to draft a plan for the city. Adopted in 1909, the **Burnham Park** called for a series of parks and artificial islands along the lakefront from Jackson Park in the south to Lincoln Park in the north. Most of the islands remained on the drawing board (**Meigs Field**, the private landing strip south of the Adler Planetarium, is the only vestige of that part of the plan) but the big idea survived, proving the truth of Burnham's famous sermon to his colleagues:

> Make no little plans; they have no magic to stir men's blood and probably themselves will not be realized. Make big plans; aim high in hope and work, remembering that a noble and logical diagram once recorded will never die, but long after we are gone will be a living thing...

Glessner family furniture and furnishings. Visit the house then stroll down the block to see the other houses in the Prairie Avenue Historic District.
✉ **1800 S Prairie Ave, The Loop** ☎ 312-326-1480 🚇 **18th St** 🚌 **1** ⏰ tours Wed-Sun 1pm, 2pm & 3pm ⑤ **$7 (free Wed)**

### Illinois Institute of Technology (3, F8)

In 1940, two engineering schools merged to form IIT. That same year, Mies van der Rohe arrived on campus from Germany. He built 22 buildings here before he retired. Crown Hall, home of the architecture department, and the Paul Galvin Library are the best of a very good lot.
✉ **S State St from 31st to 35th Sts, Near South Side** ☎ 312-567-3000 🌐 www.iit.edu 🚇 **35th/Bronzeville-IIT** 🚌 **29, 35 (or free shuttle from downtown**

campus at **565 W Adams St)** ⏰ **24-7 (best before sunset for views & security)** ⑤ **free** ♿ **good**

### Marquette Building (5, L5)

This 1893 building by Holabird & Roche is a textbook example of Chicago School construction. Large windows, made possible by steel-frame construction, bring light and air into the offices. Decoration inside and out brings light to the soul.
✉ **140 S Dearborn St, The Loop** 🚇 **Monroe** 🚌 **22, 36, 156** ⏰ **Mon-Fri 8.30am-5pm** ⑤ **free** ♿ **good**

### Monadnock Building (5, M5)

Designed by Burnham & Root in 1891, the Monadnock Building shows how high you can build a building with brick. Walls 6ft thick at the base taper gracefully as they rise, anticipating the steel-frame buildings that

the Chicago School was about to give to the world, including the 1893 addition to the south, also by Burnham & Root.
✉ **53 W Jackson Blvd, The Loop** 🚇 **Jackson, Library** 🚌 **22, 36, 156** ⏰ **Mon-Fri 8.30am-5pm** ⑤ **free** ♿ **good**

### Robie House (7, E5)

Robie House would be a masterpiece any place, anytime. On a quiet street in Hyde Park alongside the conventional houses built at the same time (Robie House was built in 1909), it is a marvel. Frank Lloyd Wright's Prairie Style masterpiece has seen some hard years, but it is being restored, and is worth the detour.
✉ **5757 S Woodlawn Ave, Hyde Park** ☎ 773-702-8374 🌐 www.wrightplus.org 🚇 **59th St** 🚌 **1, 6** ⏰ guided tours Mon-Fri 11am, noon, 1pm & 3pm, Sat & Sun 11am-3.30pm ⑤ **$9/7**

**The Rookery** (5, L4)
Pigeons from local stables gave the Rookery its name when it went up in the late 1880s. Designed by Burnham & Root, it's an archetype of pre-skyscraper design with its thick load-bearing walls. The lobby was redone by Frank Lloyd Wright in 1907 and gracefully renovated in 1992.
**✉ 209 S LaSalle St, The Loop Ⓜ Jackson, LaSalle 🚆 LaSalle 🚌 1, 7, 60, 126, 135, 136, 151, 156 ⏰ Mon-Fri 8am-6pm $ free ♿ good**

Richard Cummins
*Flock to The Rookery.*

**James R Thompson Center** (5, J4)
The architect who conceived the United Terminal at O'Hare, Helmut Jahn, designed this postmodern confection for the State of Illinois around the idea of an open plan for open government. There was a lot of trouble with the ventilation when it opened in 1986, but now it provides a great public space in the city, for visitors and workers alike.
**✉ 100 W Randolph St, The Loop ☎ 312-814-6667 Ⓜ Clark 🚆 Northwestern 🚌 22, 24, 156 ⏰ Mon-Fri 8.30am-6pm $ free ♿ excellent**

**Tribune Tower** (5, H6)
The Tribune Tower is a classic 1920s skyscraper, a steel tower costumed in a Gothic revival dress. It's endearing in the same way as the wedding cake fantasy of the Wrigley Building across the street. Stones from structures around the world decorate the facade.
**✉ 435 N Michigan Ave, Near North ☎ 312-222-3914 Ⓜ Grand 🚌 3, 145, 146, 147, 151, 157 ⏰ Mon-Fri 8.30am-5pm $ free ♿ good**

**The Wrigley Building** (5, H6) We all respect the Mies van der Rohe towers on the lakeshore, but we all love the Wrigley Building, the antithesis of what Mies stood for. It's frilly, it's white, it's happy like a fantasy castle by the Disney people.
**✉ 400 N Michigan Ave, Near North ☎ 312-644-2121 Ⓜ Grand 🚌 3, 145, 146, 147, 151, 157 ⏰ Mon-Fri 8.30am-5pm $ free ♿ good**

Richard Cummins
*James R Thompson Center: open space for open government*

# MUSEUMS

### Chicago Athenaeum
(5, K6) Chicago's museum of design opened in 1988 to promote the art of design across a range of disciplines. Its suburban branch in Schaumburg and its Good Design store at its downtown location are open while the downtown exhibit space was being renovated at time of writing.
✉ 307 N Michigan Ave, The Loop ☎ 312-372-1083 e www.chi-athenaeum.org 🅜 Madison 🚇 Randolph 🚌 3, 4, 6, 145, 147, 151 🕐 Wed-Fri 11am-6pm, Sat & Sun noon-5pm
💲 $3/2 ♿ good

### Chicago Historical Society
(5, A4) A museum dedicated to what passes for the history of Chicago and Illinois, with exhibits from the permanent collection about life in the city from frontier days to the present. There are changing exhibits on the face of the city that cast new light on the work in the permanent collection.
✉ 1601 N Clark St, Lincoln Park
☎ 312-642-4600
e www.chicagohs.org 🅜 Clark/Division, Sedgwick 🚌 22, 36, 151, 156 🕐 Mon-Sat 9.30am-4.30pm, Sun noon-5pm 💲 $5/3 (free Mon) ♿ excellent

### DuSable Museum of African American History
(7, D3) Named for Chicago's first settler, mixed-race fur trader Jean Baptiste DuSable, this museum documents African American history and celebrates African American culture with permanent historic exhibits, changing art exhibits and programs such as the 'Rising Stars of Jazz' series.
✉ 740 E 56th Pl, Hyde Park ☎ 773-947-0600 e www.dusablemuseum.org 🚇 59th St 🚌 4, 6 🕐 Mon-Sat 10am-5pm, Sun noon-5pm 💲 $3/2/1 ♿ good

### Hemingway Museum
(3, D4) The Hemingway Museum is a collection of memorabilia from the early life of Oak Park's most famous son, who was born and raised right here in the neighborhood.
✉ 338 N Oak Park Ave, Oak Park ☎ 708-848-2222 🅜 Oak Park 🕐 Thurs, Fri & Sun1-5pm, Sat 10am-5pm 💲 $6/4.50

### Mexican Fine Arts Center
(3, F7) The Art Institute of the barrio combines educational facilities, a bilingual youth radio station, and exhibit spaces for a permanent collection featuring work by Mexican masters of the last 100 years, and works by modern Mexican and Mexican-American artists.
✉ 1852 W 19th St, Pilsen ☎ 312-738-1503 e www.mfacmchicago.org 🅜 18th St 🕐 Tues-Sun 10am-5pm 💲 free ♿ good

### Museum of Contemporary Art
(5, E7) This collection of paintings, sculpture, photography, video and film documenting contemporary culture since 1945, is housed in a splendid building that does justice to its site near the Water Tower.
✉ 220 E Chicago Ave, Near North
☎ 312-280-2660
e www.mcachicago.org 🅜 Chicago 🚌 3, 10, 66, 145, 146, 147, 151 🕐 Tues 10am-8pm, Wed-Sun 10am-5pm 💲 $8/5 (free Tues) ♿ good

### Museum of Contemporary Photography
(5, N6) A set of galleries operated under the aegis of Columbia College of Visual Design, this is a museum completely dedicated to photography with a 20-year track record

*DuSable Museum of African American History*

of probing photography as a medium of expression and a medium of communication. It presents changing exhibits and work from its permanent collection.

✉ 600 S Michigan Ave, South Loop
☎ 312-663-5554
e www.colum.edu/museum/mocp ⊕ Harrison
🚇 Van Buren 🚌 1, 22, 29, 62, 145, 146, 147, 151
🕐 Mon-Fri 10am-5pm (Thurs to 8pm), Sat noon-5pm (closed holidays & Aug) ⓢ free ♿ good

## Newberry Library

(5, D4) A privately endowed collection for the humanities, open to anyone 16 and over. It's best known these days among genealogists, both for its own records and for records available through its partnership with the Family History Library in Utah. Also known for its 'Meet the Author' programs that have featured writers such as Peter Carey and Ha Jin.

✉ 60 W Walton St, Near North
☎ 312-943-9090
e www.newberry.org
⊕ Clark/Division, Chicago 🚌 22
🕐 Tues-Thurs 10am-6pm, Fri & Sat 9am-5pm ⓢ free ♿ good

## Oriental Institute Museum (7, E4)

The showcase of the Oriental Institute at the University of Chicago is dedicated to the ancient civilizations of the Middle East. At the time of writing it was being renovated, but the artefacts on view in the Egyptian and Persian Galleries are worth a stop.

✉ 1155 E 58th St, Hyde Park
☎ 773-702-9514

e www.oi.uchicago.edu
🚇 59th St 🚌 6
🕐 Tues 10am-4pm, Wed 10am-8.30pm, Thurs-Sat 10am-4pm, Sun noon-4pm
ⓢ free ♿ good

## David & Alfred Smart Museum of Art (7, D4)

The art museum of the University of Chicago is housed in a modern set of galleries at the northern end of the campus. In typical University of Chicago style, it presents exhibits with a theme, such as the recent examination of 'The Theatrical Baroque.' Always challenging, if not always easily comprehensible.

✉ 5550 S Greenwood Ave, Hyde Park
☎ 773-702-0200
e smartmuseum.uchicago.edu 🚇 59th St
🚌 6 🕐 Tues-Fri 10am-4pm (Thurs to 9pm), Sat & Sun noon-4pm
ⓢ free ♿ good

## Spertus Museum

(5, N6) Permanent exhibits from the Spertus Institute collection of Judaica and changing exhibits of artifacts and documents illustrating Jewish life and customs, present and past.

✉ 618 S Michigan Ave, South Loop ☎ 312-922-9012 e www.spertus.edu ⊕ Harrison
🚌 1, 22, 29, 62, 145, 146, 147, 151 🕐 Sun-Wed 10am-5pm, Thurs 10am-8pm, Fri 10am-3pm ⓢ $5/3 ♿ good

## Swedish American Museum Center (3, B7)

Swedish and Swedish American culture are on display in this small museum in the heart of Andersonville. There's a permanent exhibit,

'The Dream of America,' about the immigrant experience and four changing exhibits a year on art, culture and tradition.

✉ 5211 N Clark St, Andersonville
☎ 773-728-8111
e www.samac.org
⊕ Berwyn 🚌 22
🕐 Tues-Fri 10am-4pm, Sat & Sun 10am-3pm
ⓢ $4/2/1 ♿ good

## Free Times

Some of the best things in life are free, including the following:

- **Adler Planetarium**
  Tues
- **Art Institute**
  Tues
- **Field Museum**
  Wed
- **Museum of Science & Industry**
  Thurs
- **Shedd Aquarium**
  basic admission free Mon & Tues Sept-Feb
- **Terra Museum**
  Tues

## Terra Museum of American Art (5, F6)

American impressionists and works by other American painters such as Winslow Homer, John Singer Sargent and Mary Cassat, are displyed in an intimate setting in the middle of the Magnificent Mile.

✉ 664 N Michigan Ave, Near North ☎ 312-664-3939 e www.terramuseum.org ⊕ Chicago (Red) 🚌 3, 11, 125, 145, 146, 147, 151
🕐 Tues 10am-8pm, Wed-Sat 10am-6pm, Sun noon-5pm ⓢ $7/3.50 (free Tues) ♿ good

# GALLERIES

## Jean Albano Gallery
(5, F3) One of River North's best-known sources for contemporary paintings, sculpture and constructions. You may not appreciate everything you see but you will appreciate the opportunity to get close to the cutting-edge.
✉ 215 W Superior St, River North ☎ 312-440-0770 e www.jean albanogallery.com
🚇 Chicago (Brown)
🚌 66, 156 ⏰ Tues-Fri 10am-5pm, Sat 11am-5pm ⓢ free

## Architech (5, F3)
A gallery dedicated to architectural art in a city dedicated to its architecture. Changing exhibits, such as a recent show on 'The Perfect Chair' featuring chairs and drawings about chairs from famous chair designers and contemporary Chicago architects.
✉ 730 N Franklin St, Suite 200, River North
☎ 312-475-1290
🚇 Chicago (Brown)
🚌 66, 156
⏰ Thurs-Sat noon-6pm
ⓢ free ♿ good

## Baby it's Cold Outside
It can be cold and nasty in Chicago almost any time of the year. Some of our favorite strategies for dealing with the cold include:

- Buy a transit pass. If you're going to be around for any length of time, a three-, five- or seven-day bus pass will let you board the next warm, dry bus or walk down the State St subway platform (it extends the length of The Loop from Lake St past Jackson Blvd) instead of walking down State St in the rain.
- Use the Pedway, below, a set of underground passages downtown that runs more or less parallel to Randolph St from the Illinois Center, through Marshall Field's and past the Washington St subway stations to City Hall and the Thompson Center.
- Seek shelter on El platforms. Most have waiting areas with wind screens and heat lamps to take the edge off. Hit the button for heat.
- Mall walking. If the forecast says thundershowers, it might be just the time for a trip down Michigan Ave.

Raymond Hillstrom

## Douglas Dawson Gallery (5, F3)
Like an anthropology museum with discreet price tags, this selection has non-Western, mainly tribal art objects such as textiles, ceramics and furnishings, from the recent or ancient past. Nothing is new but everything is fresh.
✉ 222 W Huron St, River North ☎ 312-751-1961 e www .douglasdawson.com
🚇 Chicago (Brown)
🚌 66, 156 ⏰ Tues-Fri 10am-5.30pm, Sat 10am-5pm ⓢ free

## Carol Ehlers Gallery
(5, F3) A museum-quality collection of vintage and contemporary photography, showing everything from Steichen and Stiegliz and Strand to William Wegman's Weimaraners. A mandatory stop for fans of photography.
✉ 750 N Orleans St, River North ☎ 312-642-8611 e www.ehlers gallery.com 🚇 Chicago (Brown) 🚌 66, 156
⏰ Tues-Fri 10am-5pm, Sat 11am-5pm
ⓢ free ♿ good

## Wally Findlay Galleries (5, D6)
One of the oldest art galleries in the US. Known for impressionist and postimpressionist paintings, it's also a source for contemporary American and European works.
✉ 188 E Walton St, Near North ☎ 312-649-1500 e www.wallyfindlaygal leries.com 🚇 Chicago (Red) ⏰ Mon-Fri 10am-6pm, Sat 10am-5pm
ⓢ free ♿ good

**Illinois Art Gallery**
(5, J4) A nonprofit gallery on the 2nd floor of the Thompson Center, dedicated to presenting work by Illinois artists with changing exhibits that have included Moholy Nagy's designs and Depression-era work by WPA (Works Progress Administration) artists.
✉ James R Thompson Center, 100 W Randolph St, The Loop ☎ 312-814-3471 🚇 Clark 🚌 22, 36, 156 ⏰ Mon-Fri 9am-5pm 💲 free ♿ excellent

**Alan Koppel Gallery**
(5, E6) A small exhibit space about a quarter of the way up the John Hancock Center, featuring modern and contemporary art and mid-century French and Italian furniture.
✉ John Hancock Center, Suite 2850, 875 N Michigan Ave, Near North ☎ 312-640-0730 🌐 www.artnet.com/koppel.html 🚇 Chicago (Red) 🚌 145, 146, 151, 157 ⏰ Tues-Sat 10am-5.30pm 💲 free

**Ann Nathan Gallery**
(5, F3) Contemporary art and work that crosses the line between arts and crafts. There is an emphasis on the representational but the work on display also borders at times on the abstract.
✉ 218 W Superior St, River North ☎ 312-664-6622 🚇 Chicago (Brown) 🚌 66, 156 ⏰ Tues-Fri 10am-5.30pm, Sat 11am-5pm 💲 free ♿ good

**printworks** (5, F3)
If it goes down on paper, you'll find it here – prints, drawings, photographs and books from contemporary artists, some local and some not. A recent show featured identically sized self-portraits from scores of artists, displayed like a row of mug shots. The quality of the commentary complements the range and quality of the work.
✉ 311 W Superior St, River North ☎ 312-664-9407 🚇 Chicago (Brown) 🚌 66, 156 ⏰ Tues-Sat 11am-5pm 💲 free

**Zolla-Lieberman Gallery** (5, F3)
One of the first galleries to open in River North (back in 1976) and still a fixture in the contemporary art scene in Chicago.
✉ 325 W Huron St, River North ☎ 312-944-1990 🌐 www.zollaliebermangallery.com 🚇 Chicago (Brown) 🚌 66, 156 ⏰ Tues-Sat 10am-5.30pm 💲 free ♿ good

# PUBLIC ART

It's no surprise to find great public art in a city with great public buildings. The Loop in particular has a wealth of sculpture.

**Dawn Shadows** (5, K4)
This 1983 steel construction by Louise Nevelson looks wonderfully appropriate tucked between an office building and the El tracks on the west side of The Loop.
✉ Madison St (near Wells St), The Loop 🚇 Washington (Brown) 🚌 22, 156, 157 ⏰ 24-7 💲 free ♿ good

**Flamingo** (5, L5)
Alexander Calder's sweeping red arches are a perfect counterpoint to the restrained black buildings of Mies van der Rohe's

'On our block all the guys call her Flamingo.'

Federal Center.
✉ Chicago Federal Center, Dearborn St (btw Adams St & Jackson Blvd), The Loop 🚇 Jackson 🚌 22, 36, 151 ⏰ 24-7 💲 free ♿ good

Miro's Chicago

## The Four Seasons

(5, L5) A massive mosaic mural by Marc Chagall that dominates the plaza of the First National Bank building. It recently got a cap to protect it from the Chicago elements, which should preserve it for years to come.
✉ First National Bank of Chicago Bldg, Dearborn St (btw Madison & Monroe Sts), The Loop ⊖ Monroe
🚌 6, 22, 36, 156
🕐 24-7 ⑤ free ♿ good

## Michigan Ave Bridge

(5, H6) The friezes that decorate the piers of the Michigan Ave Bridge are an exercise in grand history art, depicting scenes from Chicago's past including the founding of Fort Dearborn at what is now the southeast corner of Michigan Ave and Wacker Dr.
✉ Michigan Ave at Wacker Dr, The Loop
⊖ State, Lake
🚌 3, 6, 145, 146, 147, 151, 157 🕐 24-7
⑤ free ♿ good

## Miro's Chicago (5, K5)

The quiet companion to the Picasso statue across the street, *Miro's Chicago* was designed in 1969 and finally constructed in 1979. The bold colors and linear shapes are a refreshing contrast to its monochromatic neighbors to the north.
✉ 69 W Washington Blvd, The Loop
⊖ Washington (Brown, Red or Blue), Clark
🚌 6, 22, 36, 156
🕐 24-7 ⑤ free ♿ good

## 'The Picasso' (5, K5)

The statue that put public art on the map in Chicago, built of the same Cor-Ten steel as the Daley Center building it decorates. When it was unveiled, then-mayor Jane Byrne looked and said, 'Well, it takes my mind off the Cubs.'
✉ Richard J Daley Center, Washington Blvd (btw Dearborn & Clark Sts), The Loop
⊖ Washington (Brown, Red or Blue), Clark
🚌 6, 22, 36, 156
🕐 24-7 ⑤ free ♿ good

## Sitting Lincoln (5, M7)

This is one of the two great Saint-Gaudens statues of Illinois's most famous son (the other, the Standing Lincoln, is in the south end of Lincoln Park, see p. 22).
✉ Congress Pkwy (btw Michigan Ave & Columbus Dr)
⊖ Library, Harrison
🚆 Van Buren
🚌 1, 3, 4, 6
🕐 7am-11pm
⑤ free ♿ good

## Tin Man (4, E3)

John Kearney, the artist who built this shiny aluminum memorial to the character from the *Wizard of Oz*, has smaller sculptures of animals in unlikely places all around the North Side. He's reputed to be one of Richard M Daley's favorite artists, so expect more of Kearney's work in the future.
✉ Oz Park, Lincoln Ave at Webster Ave, Lincoln Park ⊖ Fullerton
🚌 8, 11
🕐 sunrise to sunset
⑤ free ♿ good

'The Picasso' led the way for public art in Chicago.

# PARKS & GARDENS

### Brookfield Zoo (3, F3)
The Brookfield Zoo has over 2800 animals in reconstructions of natural habitats ranging from the Illinois prairies to the African savannahs. It also has dolphin and reptile shows for visitors seeking structured entertainment. It's open year-round, though there's more to see in warm weather.

✉ 8400 W 31st St, Brookfield ☎ 708-485-0263 e www.brookfieldzoo.org 🚊 Zoo Stop/Hollywood 🚌 PACE routes 304, 331 🚆 Eisenhower Expwy (I-290) west from The Loop about 14 miles to 1st Ave ⏱ summer 9.30am-6pm; winter 10am-5pm; spring & fall Mon-Fri 10am-5pm, Sat & Sun 10am-6pm; ⑤ $7/3.50 (free Tues & Thurs Oct-Mar); children's zoo $1/50¢; under 2s free ♿ excellent

### Chicago Botanic Garden (1, B2)
The Chicago Botanic Garden is well worth the 20-mile drive from the city center. Operated by the Chicago Horticultural Society with cooperation from the Chicago Park District, it consists of 23 gardens over 300 acres, including an open prairie garden, a children's garden, a Japanese garden and an evergreen garden (for those winter months). ✉ 1000 Lake-Cook Rd, near Edens Expwy, Glencoe ☎ 847-835-5440 e www.chicago-botanic.org 🚊 Braeside 🚆 Kennedy Expwy

*A welcome break: Chicago Botanic Garden*

Raymond Hillstrom

(I-94) north to Edens Expwy (I-94) to Lake-Cook Rd exit ⏱ 8am-sunset (closed Christmas Day) ⑤ free, parking $4 ♿ good

### Garfield Park Conservatory (3, E6)
The big sister of the Lincoln Park Conservatory has six large rooms under glass, a children's center, an exhibit hall and an outdoor sensory garden. Built in 1907, it was a showpiece of the West Side. It's getting a makeover now, including its own stop on the Green Line, which should open in 2002. ✉ 300 N Central Park Ave, Garfield Park ☎ 312-746-5100 e www.garfield-conservatory.org 🚌 Free Conservatory Trolley from Chicago Omni, Chicago Cultural Center & Chicago Hilton Towers ⏱ 9am-5pm; 9am-8pm during Celebration in Lights end Nov to Jan 6 ⑤ free ♿ good

### Jackson Park (7, E7)
Jackson Park was the site of the Columbian Exposition of 1893. It's home to the Museum of

Science & Industry and the Osaka Garden, both built for the Exposition. Recreation facilities include a golf course, a yacht club, several beaches, playing fields and a nature pre-serve popular with birders. ✉ bounded by 56th St, Stony Island Ave & 67th St, Hyde Park ☎ 312-747-6187 🚊 59th St 🚌 1, 6, 10 ⏱ 7am-11pm ⑤ free ♿ good

### Morton Arboretum (1, D1)
The Morton Arboretum is a 1700-acre park in the far western suburbs, with over 25 miles of trails, more miles of roads and a splendid collection of trees and plants from native species to the exotic. Come for hiking, for birdwatching or for exposure to the latest in plant research. ✉ Rte 53 north of I-88, Lisle ☎ 630-719-2400 e www.mortonarb.org 🚆 Eisenhower Expwy (I-290) west from The Loop to I-88, west on I-88 past I-395 interchange to Rte 53 ⏱ 7am-7pm, Nov-Mar to 5pm ⑤ $6/car ($3 Wed) ♿ excellent

### Oz Park (4, E3)

L Frank Baum lived nearby, so it shouldn't be a surprise to see statues of the Tin Man and the Cowardly Lion by local artist John Kearney in this gracious neighborhood park at the beginning of a yellow brick road leading into the park, towards the dog walk, picnic grounds and playing fields that keep this place busy all day long.
✉ **bounded by Webster Ave, Larrabee St, Dickens Ave & Halsted St, Lincoln Park** ☎ **312-747-2200** Ⓣ **Armitage, Fullerton** 🚌 **8, 11** ⏲ **sunrise to sunset** ⑤ **free** ♿ **good**

### Wicker Park (2, E4)

This little triangle near the six-point intersection of Milwaukee, North and Damen Aves houses a memorial to Lucy Parsons, a 19th-century anarchist and labor organizer, one of the rare monuments to a woman in Chicago.
✉ **bounded by Wicker Park Ave, Damen Ave & Schiller St, Wicker Park** ☎ **312-742-7583** Ⓣ **Damen (Blue)** 🚌 **56, 72** ⏲ **7am-11pm** ⑤ **free** ♿ **good**

# COLLEGES & UNIVERSITIES

### DePaul University

**(4, E2)** The largest Catholic university in the US was founded by Vincentian fathers in 1898 to teach the children of immigrants. It's still teaching the children of the area, along with lots of middle-class kids from the suburbs, today. The main campus in Lincoln Park sits on 36 of the nicer acres on the North Side.
✉ **2320 N Kenmore Ave, Lincoln Park** ☎ **312-362-6709** ⓔ **www.depaul.edu** Ⓣ **Fullerton** 🚌 **8, 11, 74** ⏲ **phone for campus tours** ⑤ **free** ♿ **good**

### Moody Bible Institute

**(5, E4)** Founded by DL Moody as the Chicago Evangelical Society in 1886, the Moody Bible Institute has been training ministers and missionaries ever since from this location near the fleshpots of Rush St.
✉ **820 N LaSalle St, Near North** ☎ **312-329-4000** ⓔ **www.moody.edu** Ⓣ **Chicago (Brown or Red)** 🚌 **22, 156** ⏲ **museum Mon-Fri 8.30am-4.30pm, tours in summer Mon-Fri 11am & 2pm** ⑤ **free** ♿ **good**

'Give me a D!' DePaul University gets some support.

### Northwestern University (1, C3)

The main campus of the only private institution in the Big 10 Conference is just north of downtown Evanston on the North Shore. The lakeside campus is filled with beautiful Gothic-revival buildings from the 1910s and 20s.
✉ **Sheridan Rd at Chicago Ave, Evanston** ☎ **847-491-3741** ⓔ **www.northwestern.edu** Ⓣ **Davis, Foster** 🚌 **Davis** ⏲ **campus tours Mon-Fri 9.15am & 1.15pm (July-late Aug); Sat 10.30am & 11.45am (Oct-late Dec); 11.45am (Jan-Apr)** ⑤ **free** ♿ **good**

### University of Illinois at Chicago (3, E7)

Called the Chicago Circle campus when it opened in the 1960s, after the circular freeway interchange to the northeast, this is the concrete monster that ate the Near West Side slums, including the original Maxwell St Market where immigrant Jews once trundled pushcarts. Today it has 25,000 students, mostly commuters, and 200 buildings on 80 acres.
✉ **11th fl, 1200 W Harrison St, Near West Side** ☎ **312-996-4350** ⓔ **www.uic.edu** Ⓣ **Halsted/U of I** ⏲ **tours Mon-Fri 2-3pm** ⑤ **free** ♿ **good**

# PLACES OF WORSHIP

## Bahá'í House of Worship (1, B3)

The Bahá'í Temple is a dream of the Arabian Nights transported to the genteel streets of the North Shore. Built in the 1920s it is now the oldest standing Bahá'í house of worship in the world. Its pearly white walls and dome are inscribed inside and out with verses from Bahá'í writings and surrounded by acres of glorious gardens.

✉ 100 Linden Ave, Wilmette ☎ 847-853-2300 🚇 Linden 🚋 Lake Shore Dr north from city to Sheridan Rd, north on Sheridan through Evanston, past Northwestern University to Linden Ave ⏲ 10am-5pm; summer (mid-May to early Sept) 10am-10pm ⑤ free ♿ good

*Bahá'í Temple: a taste of the East in the Midwest*

Richard Cummins

## Chicago Loop Synagogue (5, K4)

The interior of this synagogue is filled with light from a 30ft x 40ft wall of stained glass by American artist Abraham Rattner, entitled 'Let There Be Light and There Was Light.'

✉ 16 S Clark St, The Loop ☎ 312-346-7370 🚇 Monroe 🚌 22, 24, 36 ⏲ Mon-Fri 9am-4.30pm ⑤ free ♿ good

## Holy Name Cathedral

(5, F5) This smallish Roman Catholic church is home of the archdiocese of Chicago, one of the largest in the country. Come in for a respite from the commotion of the Near North Side or to enjoy the music when the choir is practising.

✉ 735 N State St, Near North ☎ 312-787-8040 🚇 Chicago (Red) 🚌 36 ⏲ 5.30am-7pm ⑤ free ♿ good

## Midwest Buddhist Temple (4, F4)

This Japanese-American confection sits incongruously in the middle of the brick and clapboard cottages of the Old Town Triangle near Lincoln Park. The temple complex is generally not open to the public, but it's worth a walk around if you're in the area.

✉ 435 W Menomonee St, Old Town ☎ 312-943-7801 🚇 Sedgwick ⏲ school and group tours only, by prior arrangement ⑤ free ♿ good

## Moody Church (5, A4)

The idea that one can find, let alone fill, an evangelical Protestant church with 4000 seats in the city of Chicago gives you a good idea just how the big the city is. There are no columns to impede the view, ideal for congregants and ideal for television cameras (services are broadcast far and wide).

✉ 1630 N Clark St, Old Town ☎ 312-943-0466 🚇 Sedgwick 🚌 72 ⏲ Mon-Fri 8.30am-5pm ⑤ free ♿ good

## St Michael's Church

(4, G3) This is the mother church of the German Catholic community, rebuilt after the Chicago Fire in a rococo style imported from Munich and Dresden. It's bigger, taller and grander than Holy Name, reflecting the success of the Germans who settled the North Side.

✉ 1633 N Cleveland Ave, Old Town ☎ 312-642-2498 🚇 Sedgwick 🚌 72 ⏲ Mon-Fri 9am-8.30pm, Sat 9am-noon ⑤ free ♿ no

## Unity Temple (3, D4)

Frank Lloyd Wright designed this Unitarian Church at the turn of the 20th century. The design is remarkably fresh today, though the building itself needs some work (like so many of Wright's buildings, whether old or relatively new). No steeple, no spires, just beautiful tranquil spaces to contemplate your place in the universe.

✉ 875 W Lake St, Oak Park ☎ 708-383-8873 e www.unitytemple-utrf.org 🚇 Oak Park 🚌 Oak Park ⏲ 1-4pm, Memorial Day-Labor Day 10am-5pm ⑤ $4 Mon-Fri, $6 Sat & Sun (guided tours $6 extra) ♿ good

# QUIRKY CHICAGO

## Body Slices (7, D7)
In 1943, a male and a female cadaver were sliced up (one vertically, one on the horizontal), frozen and put on display in the MSI. They're still there, tucked away on a landing far from the cafeteria.

✉ Museum of Science & Industry, 5700 S Lake Shore Dr, Hyde Park ☎ 800-468-6674, 773-684-1414 ✉ www.msichicago.org ▣ 59th St ▣ 6, 10 ⊘ Memorial Day-Labor Day & school holidays 9am-5.30pm; off-season Mon-Fri 9.30am-4pm, Sat & Sun 9.30am-5.30pm ⑤ $9/5 (Omnimax screenings additional) ♿ excellent

## Brew & View (4, C2)
Chicagoans like beer and Chicagoans like movies. The people at the Vic Theater, a movie palace from the 1920s, figured a way to do both at once. They ripped out the orchestra seats to make room for tables and chairs, then put in three bars so movie-goers can get another pitcher without missing a thing.

✉ 3145 N Sheffield St, Lakeview ☎ 773-472-0449 ⊖ Belmont ▣ 8, 77 ⊘ box office Mon-Fri noon-6pm, Sat 10am-4pm ⑤ varies ♿ good

## Challenge Park Xtreme (1, 1E)
If you ever wanted to star in your own war flick, this is the place. There are 150 acres just for paintball firefights – fields and woods with a fort and a six-square block bit of cityscape where you can re-enact the Battle of the Bulge.

✉ 2903 Schweitzer Rd, Joliet ☎ 815-726-2800 ✉ www.challengepark.com ▣ Stevenson Expwy (I-55) to I-80 east to State Rte 53 south to Larraway Rd, right on Larraway Rd to Patterson Rd, left on Patterson Rd to Schweitzer Rd ⊘ Apr-Nov Wed 10am-6pm, Thurs & Fri 10am-10pm, Sat 9am-10pm, Sun 9am-6pm; Dec-Mar Wed-Fri 10am-5pm, Sat & Sun 9am-5pm ⑤ admission $10, air gun rental and 100 paintballs $22 total

## Cubs Shrine (4, B2)
This modest house across from Wrigley Field is a shrine to the Cubs raised to the level of folk art.

✉ 1100 W Addison St, Wrigleyville ⊖ Addison ▣ 22, 36 ⑤ free ♿ good

## Diversey Driving Range (4, D4)
It's a long, dark winter, so the Chicago Park District has gone the extra mile for city golfers by building a set of heated stations at the Diversey Driving Range in Lincoln Park. 'Heated tees offer golfers the opportunity to keep their game sharp year-round,' says Chicago Park District Superintendent David Doig.

✉ 141 W Diversey Pkwy, Lincoln Park ☎ 312-742-7929 ⊖ Diversey ▣ 151, 156 ⊘ 7am-10pm ⑤ $7/bucket of golf balls, $60/10 bucket debit card ♿ good

## Division St Russian & Turkish Baths (3, D7)
The place to *schvitz* (sweat) like they do in Russia. Separate facilities for men and women, with snacks and sandwiches at the counters in the locker room just like the old country. You want some smoked fish with your steam? Cash only.

✉ 1914 W Division St, Ukrainian Village ☎ 773-384-9671 ⊖ Division ▣ 50, 70 ⊘ 8am-10pm ⑤ $17 (massage extra)

*For when the family is driving you mad.*

## Family Golf Center (5, J8)
A nine-hole, par-three course and driving range, tucked in an open-air pit under the towers of the Illinois Center north of Grant Park. The course is open April to October. The driving range is open year-round.

✉ 221 N Columbus Dr, The Loop ☎ 312-616-1234 ▣ Randolph ▣ 60, 4 ⊘ Apr-Oct 7am-9pm, Nov-Mar 10am-6pm (driving range only); course closes at sunset ⑤ $15/round, $15/6 driving range ♿ good

### International Museum of Surgical Science

**(5, A5)** This Gold Coast mansion owned by the International College of Surgeons houses a permanent collection of surgical instruments through the ages and changing exhibits that probe the intersections between art and medicine. Perfect for young children of any age.

✉ 1524 N Lake Shore Dr, Gold Coast
☎ 312-642-6502
Ⓜ Clark/Division
🚌 151
🕐 Tues-Sat 10am-4pm
💲 $5/3

### Leather Archive & Museum **(3, A7)**

Chicago hosts the International Mr Leather contest every Memorial Day so it's natural that the city would be the home to this collection of books, photographs and documents of and for the leather/S&M/fetish community. Mapplethorpe photos and much, much more.

✉ 6418 W Greenview Ave at W Devon, W Rogers Park
☎ 773-761-9200
Ⓜ Loyola 🚌 22, 36
🕐 Thurs 2-8pm, first Sat of the month noon-5pm, other hours by appointment 💲 free

### Old St Patrick's Church Block Party

**(5, L1)** This parish on the edge of The Loop throws the world's largest block party each year, originally conceived as a way for Catholic singles to meet one another. Both the party and the marriages that follow have become local traditions.

✉ 700 W Adams St, West Loop
☎ 312-648-1021
Ⓜ Quincy, Clinton
🚇 Union
🚌 156
🕐 3rd weekend of July
💲 free ♿ good

## FOR CHILDREN

All the major museums have special children's programs. The Art Institute even has a separate entrance in the back for school buses and folding stools for children to use on docent tours.

### Chicago Playworks for Families & Young Audiences **(5, N6)**

Chicago Playworks was founded as the Goodman Children's Theater in 1925, and is now run by the DePaul University theater department. It presents three shows a year at the Merle Ruskin Theater in The Loop. The 2001 offerings were 'Charlie and the Chocolate Factory,' 'Junglebook' and 'Duke Kahanamoku v the Surf Nappers.'

✉ 60 E Balbo Dr, The Loop ☎ 312-922-1999
🅔 theatreschool.de paul.edu Ⓜ Harrison
🚌 1, 22, 29, 62, 145, 146, 147, 151 🕐 phone for performance times
💲 $7/2 ♿ good

### Chicago Children's Museum **(5, G10)**

The Children's Museum is one part schoolroom and one part playroom, with a little contemporary museum commerce on the side. There are special early childhood exhibits for very small children, alongside a dinosaur exhibit, a science lab and an arts and crafts studio for older children.

✉ Navy Pier, 700 E Grand Ave, Near North

☎ 312-527-1000
🅔 www.chichildrens museum.org
🚌 124 express; 29, 56, 65, 66; 120 & 121 rush hrs only 🕐 Tues-Sun 10am-5pm (8pm Thurs), open Mon school holidays 10am-5pm
💲 $6.50/5.50 (families free Thurs 5-8pm)
♿ good

Chicago Children's Museum: a world of fun for the kids

Raymond Hillstrom

**Dave & Busters** (5, D4)
A little bit of Las Vegas on the Near North Side, a huge arcade with low-tech and hi-tech games and simple food for the whole family. It also has alcohol for parents who need a good stiff drink late in the afternoon. Kids disappear like Cinderella's carriage every night at 10.
✉ 1030 N Clark St, Gold Coast ☎ 312-943-5151 ⊖ Clark/Division ☒ 22 ⏰ Mon-Thurs 11.30am-1am, Fri & Sat 11.30am-2am, Sun 11.30am-midnight ⑤ $5 after 10pm Fri & Sat, otherwise free ♿ good

**DisneyQuest** (5, G6)
Who needs to go to Orlando when you have over 250 rides and attractions tastefully packed into a five-floor indoor amusement park just off Michigan Ave. Shoot the rapids on a virtual cruise, spin on a cybercoaster or battle villains with a laser sword.
✉ 55 E Ohio St, Near North ☎ 312-222-1300 🌐 www.disneyquest.com ⊖ Grand (Red) ☒ 3, 36, 145, 146, 147, 151 ⏰ Sun-Wed 11am-7pm, Thurs & Fri 11am-10pm, Sat 10am-10pm ⑤ all-day pass $26, entry and pay as you go $10, late night (2hrs before closing) $13 ♿ good

*Disneyland in a box*

Richard Cummins

## More Kid's Stuff

The following attractions have special programs or exhibits for kids or are particularly kid-friendly. Also, see page 68 for children's shopping options

- **Art Institute** (p. 15)
- **Field Museum** (p. 18), below
- **Lincoln Park Zoo** (p. 22)
- **Museum of Science & Industry** (p. 24)
- **Harold G Washington Library** (p. 28)

**Farm in the Zoo** (4, F4)
This three-acre working farm at the south end of the Lincoln Park Zoo gives city kids a chance to learn that milk does not come directly out of a bottle.
✉ Lincoln Park Zoo, 2200 N Stockton Dr, Lincoln Park ☎ 312-742-2000 🌐 www.chicagoparkdistrict.com

⊖ Armitage, Fullerton ☒ 22, 36, 151 ⏰ 10am-4.30pm ⑤ free ♿ good

**Elizabeth Morse Genius Children's Garden** (3, E6)
A new botanical garden at the Garfield Park Conservatory designed specifically for kids, with

interactive exhibits to allow children to see, touch, taste and smell plants.
✉ **300 N Central Park Ave, Garfield Park** ☎ **312-746-5100** e www.garfield-conservatory.org 🚌 Free Conservatory Trolley from Chicago Omni, Chicago Cultural Center & Chicago Hilton Towers ⏲ 9am-5pm ⑤ free & good

### Old Town School of Folk Music (4, F3)

The Old Town School of Folk Music not only offers a series of classes for children that would put a conventional music school to shame but also presents a series of children's musicals every year with book, music and lyrics by Old Town School teachers. Not to be missed.
✉ **909 W Armitage Ave, Old Town** ☎ **773-728-6000** 🚇 Armitage 🚌 8, 73 ⏲ call ahead ⑤ $5/4 & good

### Puppet Parlor (3, B7)

The National Marionette Company performs original stories, adaptations of classic fairy tales and classic opera or follies for adults. The 2001 offerings were 'Jack Frost' by Pushkin and 'The Magic Flute' by Mozart.
✉ **1922 W Montrose Ave, Ravenswood** ☎ **773-774-2919** 🚇 Montrose 🚌 22, 78 ⏲ Children's performances Sat & Sun 2pm, adult performances 1pm & 8pm Wed ⑤ $14/7 & good

### Rock & Roll McDonald's (5, G4)

The Hard Rock Café goes to Hamburger U. Life-size cutouts of the greats (the Beatles, the Supremes) and rock & roll memorabilia are sure to put the happy back in 'happy meals.'
✉ **600 N Clark St, Near North** ☎ **312-664-7940** 🚇 Grand (Red) 🚌 22, 36 ⏲ 24-7 ⑤ free & good

### The Shops at North Bridge (5, H6)

The 3rd floor of the vertical mall behind the Wrigley Building is dedicated to kids. Look for the Lego Store as you get off the escalator, shop at a half-dozen or more shops from Madison & Friends to Sanrio, then get a real Chicago dog at Fluky's upstairs on level 4.
✉ **520 N Michigan Ave, Near North** ☎ **312-327-2300** 🚇 Grand (Red) 🚌 3, 36, 145, 146, 147, 151 ⏲ Mon-Sat 10am-8pm, Sun 11am-6pm ⑤ free & good

### Six Flags Great America Theme Park (1, A2)

If the kids are looking for roller coasters, a demon drop or something else to leave their stomachs in their shoes, drive north to Six Flags in Gurnee where they'll find 110 acres of thrills.
✉ **Grand Ave at Tri-State Tollway (I-94), Gurnee** ☎ **847-249-4636** e www.sixflags.com 🚌 I-94 north from Chicago about 45 mins to Grand Ave exit ⏲ open May-Oct; hours vary, generally 10am-10pm June-Aug ⑤ $39.99/19.99 (special packages for 2-day visits) & excellent

## Babysitting

Many hotels, large and small, have babysitting services for extra fees. Also try: **American Childcare Services** (☎ 312-6344-7300, e www.americanchildcare.com), which guarantees sitters if you give 24hrs notice, for a booking fee of $50 and $50/hr (4hr minimum); **North Shore Nannies** (☎ 847-864-2424), which provides nanny temps for $10/hr (4hr minimum) and booking fees from $18-40; or **American Registry of Nurses and Sitters** (☎ 773-248-8100), which provides sitters on a sliding scale starting at $12/hr for two children to $20/hr for several children. North Shore Nannies and American Registry strongly suggest advance bookings.

Tom Given

# KEEPING FIT

If you can keep an eye on the portions at dinner, it's not hard to stay fit in Chicago. Outdoors, there's everything you could ask for, save for surfing. There are rinks in winter, beaches and pools and boats in summer. There are acres of playing fields and miles of bike paths. There are dog runs and tennis courts and golf courses and driving ranges. And everything is close at hand, in the great lakefront parks and smaller neighborhood playgrounds.

Indoors, there are facilities for everyone everywhere. Every good-sized hotel has a small fitness room. Some grand hotels have grand spas. Local gyms and health clubs offer cardio machines, weight-training facilities, pools, rock-climbing walls and classes of every description.

### Bike Chicago (5, G10)

These folks rent bikes here at Navy Pier and at locations at the North Ave beach in Lincoln Park and the 63rd St beach in Jackson Park. Free guided tours of Lincoln Park, Grant Park or the Osaka Japanese Gardens in Jackson Park leave Navy Pier daily (in season) at 11.30am and 1.30pm.

✉ **Navy Pier, 600 E Grand Ave, Near North** ☎ **312-755-0488** **e** **www.bikechicago .com** 🚌 **124 express; 29, 56, 65, 66; 120 & 121 rush hrs only; free trolley from Grand St El station and cnr State & Rush Sts** ⏲ **Apr & May 9am-7pm, June-Sept 8am-10pm, Oct & Nov 9am-7pm** ⑤ **$7.75-8.75/hr, $30-35/day** ♿ **good**

### Sports Hotlines
- **Chicago Area Runners Association** ☎ 312-666-9836
- **Chicagoland Bicycle Federation** ☎ 312-427-3325
- **Chicago Park District** ☎ 312-742-7529

### Chicagoland Canoe Base (3, C6)

The North Fork of the Chicago River is pretty clean and getting cleaner. Rent a kayak or canoe here, where Irving Park Rd crosses the river, and see beavers and birds and other wildlife as you paddle upstream.

✉ **4019 N Narrangansett Ave, Ravenswood** ☎ **773-777-1489** 🚌 **80** ⏲ **Mon-Wed, Fri & Sat 9am-5pm, Thurs 9am-9pm** ⑤ **$35 1st day, $15 each additional day**

### City Sweats (4, E4)

They'll sell you a set of in-line skates here or rent you a set by the hour or the day so you can explore the trails of Lincoln Park and the streets and sidewalks of the Lincoln Park and Lakeview neighborhoods.

✉ **2467 N Clark St, Lincoln Park** ☎ **773-348-2489** 🚇 **Fullerton** 🚌 **22, 36** ⏲ **Mon-Fri 11am-8pm, Sat 10am-6pm, Sun 11am-5pm** ⑤ **$7/hr, $19/day**

### Daley Bicentennial Plaza Tennis Courts (5, K7)

These are the show courts of the city, 12 lighted courts in the middle of Grant Park open for play from April through October. Courts are first-come, first-served, so bring a book if you're an impatient type.

✉ **337 E Randolph St, Grant Park** ☎ **312-742-7529** **e** **www.chicago parkdistrict.com** 🚇 **Randolph** 🚌 **Randolph** 🚌 **60** ⏲ **7am-11pm (in season)** ⑤ **free** ♿ **good**

*Spiderman is back in town.*

### Lincoln Park Athletic Club (4, D2)

A zippy facility for Lincoln Park yuppies featuring a pool, a basketball court, cardio machines and

weight-training equipment, a full range of free classes and rock climbing on the wall in the parking lot. Massage and child care available if you're sore or tired. Friendly staff make your workout all the more enjoyable.
✉ 1019 W Diversey Pkwy, Lincoln Park
☎ 773-529-2022
🚇 Diversey 🚌 8, 76
🕐 Mon-Thurs 5am-11pm, Fri 5am-10pm, Sat & Sun 7am-9pm
💲 $14/day 🚹 good

### Sydney R Marovitz Golf Course (4, A3)
Better known as Waveland to locals in Lakeview, this nine-hole course is one of Lincoln Park's amazing amenities, offering some of the best views this side of Pebble Beach. Call ahead to reserve a time and show up a half-hour ahead to register.
✉ N Lake Shore Dr at Irving Park Rd, Wrigleyville ☎ 312-742-7930 📧 www.chic agoparkdistrict.com
🚇 Sheridan 🚌 151
🕐 sunrise to sunset
💲 nonresidents $16.50/9.25, residents $15/8.25 🚹 good

### New City YMCA
(4, G3) The New City Y has an Olympic-sized pool, the latest in workout machines and all the classes you'd expect from yoga to kick boxing to fencing.
✉ 1515 N Halsted St, Old Town/Cabrini Green
☎ 312-266-1242
📧 www.ymca.net
🚇 North/Clybourn
🚌 8, 72 🕐 Mon-Fri 5.30am-10.30pm, Sat 7am-7pm, Sun 9am-6pm 💲 $10/day
🚹 good

### Quad's (4, A3)
A serious gym for men and women serious about body building. A no-frills place where you'll see everyone from local GODS (gays on disability & steroids) to Lake Shore Dr housewives.
✉ 3727 N Broadway, Wrigleyville ☎ 773-404-7867 🚇 Addison
🚌 8, 36, 152 🕐 Mon-Fri 6am-10pm, Sat 6am-9pm, Sun 9am-8pm 💲 $10/day, $35/week

### Skate on State (5, K5)
Someday they will build on this site across from Marshall Field's in the very heart of The Loop, but until they do this is the place to skate (or watch the skaters) amid the roaring traffic's boom.
✉ 100 N State St, The Loop ☎ 312-744-3315
🚇 Washington
🚋 Randolph 🚌 6, 29, 36, 62, 146 🕐 Nov-Mar 9am-7pm 💲 free, skate rental $3/2 🚹 good

### Sweat Shop on Broadway (4, C3)
Watch most of Lakeview go by as you run on your treadmill or climb your stair machine in the front room of this comfortable neighborhood gym. Free weights, weight-training equipment and classes for men and women in addition to the cardio stuff in the window.
✉ 3217 N Broadway, Lakeview ☎ 773-871-2789 📧 www.Chicago SweatShop.com
🚇 Belmont 🚌 36, 77
🕐 Mon-Thurs 5.30am-11pm, Fri 5.30am-10pm, Sat 7am-9pm, Sun 8am-9pm
💲 $12/day 🚹 good

"I ran 50 laps...of the statue."

# out & about

## WALKING TOURS
### The Loop

From the State St El station, walk down State St past the Chicago Theater **1**, Marshall Field's **2**, the Burnham Hotel **3** and the Carson, Pirie, Scott Bldg **4** to Palmer House Hotel **5**. Walk through the concourse, detour into the lobby and head out to Wabash Ave; then turn right into Adams St. Pass Rhapsody and the Symphony Center **6** to Michigan Ave and the Art Institute entrance **7**. Walk down the west side of Michigan Ave, past the Chicago Architectural Foundation in the Santa Fe Center **8**, the Fine Arts Bldg **9** and the Auditorium Bldg **10**, then turn right

### SIGHTS & HIGHLIGHTS

Marshall Field's (p. 59)
Carson, Pirie, Scott Bldg (p. 33)
Art Institute (p. 15)
Auditorium Bldg (p. 33)
Harold G Washington Library (p. 28)
Monadnock Bldg (p. 34)
Marquette Bldg (p. 34)
*Four Seasons* (p. 40)
'The Picasso' (p. 40)
The Rookery (p. 35)
Chicago Board of Trade (p. 16)

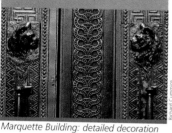

*Marquette Building: detailed decoration*

Richard Cummins

**distance** 2.5 miles (4km)
**duration** 3hrs
▶ **start** State St El (Red)
● **end** Quincy El

on Congress Pkwy and walk past the Washington Library **11** to Dearborn St. Turn right up Dearborn past the Monadnock Bldg **12**, the Federal Center **13**, the Marquette Bldg **14** and the First National Bank Bldg and the Chagall *Four Seasons* **15** to the Daley Center and 'The Picasso' **16**. From the Daley Center Plaza head west on Washington Blvd to LaSalle St and head south and look into the lobbies of The Rookery **17**, the Bank of America Bldg **18** and the CBOT Bldg **19**. Head west one block on Jackson Blvd and turn north on Wells St to the Quincy El station.

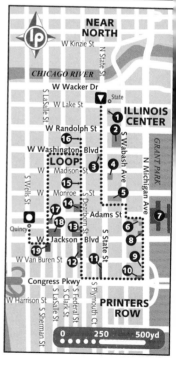

## Magnificent Mile

From the Randolph St El station walk east past the Chicago Cultural Center ❶ to Michigan Avenue and turn left. Head north past the Carbide & Carbon Bldg ❷ and over the Michigan Avenue Bridge ❸. Look at the Wrigley Bldg ❹, then cross the street and look at the stones in the facade of the Tribune Tower ❺. Continue up Michigan Avenue past the Hotel Inter-continental ❻. Cross the street again at Erie St, pass the Terra

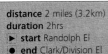

**distance** 2 miles (3.2km)
**duration** 2hrs
▶ **start** Randolph El
● **end** Clark/Division El

**SIGHTS & HIGHLIGHTS**
Chicago Cultural Center (p. 17)
Wrigley Bldg (p. 35)
Tribune Tower (p. 35)
Hotel Intercontinental (p. 103)
Terra Museum (p. 37)
Water Tower Place (p. 61)
John Hancock Center (p. 21)
900 N Michigan Ave (p. 60)
Bloomingdales (p. 59)

*Water Tower adds yet more class to Mag Mile.*

Museum ❼ and continue past the Water Tower ❽ and the Fourth Presbyterian Church, where you can stop to take in the plaza and the tower of the John Hancock Center across the street (once the tallest, still one of the best in town) . Bring your eyes back to street level, and head north again to 900 N Michigan Avenue and Bloomingdale's ❾. Duck into the mall for a look, then continue north to Oak St. Turn left into Oak, past Barneys ❿ to Rush St. Walk up Rush to where it merges with State St, continue on State to Division and turn left again to the El station at Clark and Division.

## Wicker Park

From the Damen El station walk north to the six-point intersection of Damen, Milwaukee and North Aves and turn left (north) into Milwaukee Ave. Head two blocks to Caton St and turn left again. Take Caton to Leavitt St and turn left, heading south on Leavitt across North Ave to Pierce Ave. Turn left on Pierce to Hoyne Ave then turn right on Hoyne and take Hoyne to Schiller St. Make a left on Schiller and cross Damen. Look at the mansion at 1941 Schiller ❶ then turn into Wicker Park to visit the Lucy Parsons memorial ❷ on the Damen Ave side opposite LeMoyne St. Cross Damen and head north to the viaduct at Bloomingdale Ave, looking into the windows at MOD ❸, and Commune ❹ as you go. Cross the

Anything is possible in Wicker Park.

Tom Given

street and walk back to Milwaukee, passing the Red Dog and the Border Tap ❺. Walk down the east side of Milwaukee to Evergreen and then the other side back to Damen and the El, passing the Bongo Room ❻ and the Double Door ❼ on the way.

**distance** 2 miles (3.2km)
**duration** 2hrs
▶ **start** Damen El
● **end** Damen El

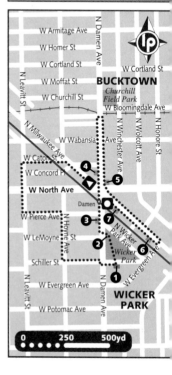

# Hyde Park

From the bus stop in front of the Museum of Science & Industry ❶ take 57th St west under the viaduct to Kimbark Ave. Turn left on Kimbark and head south one block to 58th St, turn right and go one block to Robie House ❷ at the corner of Woodlawn Ave. Turn south on

## SIGHTS & HIGHLIGHTS

Robie House (p. 34)
University of Chicago (p. 31)

University of Chicago overplays the ivy card.

Woodlawn to the Rockefeller Memorial Chapel ❸ at the corner of 59th St and stop in for a look. From the chapel continue west on 59th St to the entrance to the Main Quadrangle of the University of Chicago, past University Ave. Walk into the quad and bear left to the Bond Chapel ❹, which is tucked back in the southwest corner. Head back into the main quad and head north to 57th St. Turn right past the Hutchinson Commons ❺ and continue east on 57th St back under the viaduct to the corner of Stony Island Ave where you can pick up the No 6 Jeffrey bus at the stop on the southeast corner.

**distance** 2.5 miles (4km)  **duration** 3hrs
▶ **start** No 6 bus stop at Museum of Science & Industry
● **end** No 6 bus stop at 57th St & Stony Island Ave

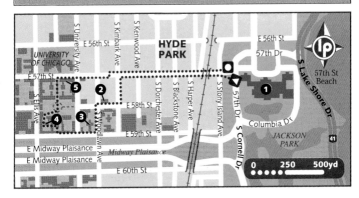

# EXCURSIONS
## Oak Park                                                    (1, C2)

This quiet suburb eight miles west of The Loop is the birthplace of a revolutionary in the field of writing (Ernest Hemingway) and a revolution in the field of architecture (this is where Frank Lloyd Wright hit his stride).

### INFORMATION

*10 miles west of Chicago*

🚇 Green Line to Oak Park Station or Metra from Union Station to Oak Park Station ☎ 708-848-1500

ⓘ Oak Park Visitors Center, 158 Forest Ave

🕐 10am-4pm

✗ Peterson's Emporium (1100 Chicago Ave; ☎ 708-386-6131)

No steeples or spires at the Unity Temple

Take the Green Line through the shambles of Chicago's West Side to the Oak Park station, walk north up Oak Park Ave to Lake St, enter a small Midwest town and begin to appreciate the full scale of their respective achievements.

Wright's achievements are all around you as you head west along Lake past his Unity Temple (see p. 43) and north along Forest Ave to his home and studio (see p. 30). When most of the good citizens of Oak Park were building tall frame houses with gables and turrets that just scream 'Teddy Roosevelt,' Wright convinced over 20 of his neighbors to build long, low brick houses. These Prairie Style homes look almost contemporary even after almost a century.

Hemingway's achievement is invisible, but as you wander the quiet streets past the houses where he was born and raised and examine the relics in the Hemingway Museum (see p. 36) consider how far he ran to get away from this too-comfortable home.

Moore House exemplifies the Prairie Style homes of Oak Park.

## North Shore    (1, B3)

Take a spin up the North Shore and take in one of the longest stretches of the loveliest suburbia the world has to offer.

This is John Hughes land, a world of tree-lined streets, astonishing public schools and libraries, and rambling houses and well-groomed teenagers struggling with adolescence. It's the great payoff of Burnham's grand plan to preserve the lakefront.

Northwestern University, on the lakefront, lends downtown Evanston a college town air, while the Bahá'í House of Worship (p. 43) calls forth notions of Arabian Nights.

## INFORMATION

*70 miles north of Chicago*

🚗 Take Sheridan Road north from the end of Lake Shore Dr in Lincoln Park, to Deerpath Road in Lake Forest. Take Deerpath Rd west to the Edens Expressway (I-94). Turn south on the Edens to Lake-Cook Road exit. Head east on Lake-Cook past the Chicago Botanic Garden (see p. 41) to Green Bay Rd. Turn on Green Bay Rd to Willow Rd in Winnetka, then turn right and take Willow back to the Edens, and continue south to the city

✕ Buon Giorno (566 Chestnut St, Winnetka; ☎ 847-784-8899)

## Indiana Dunes   (1, D5)

The Burnham Plan for Chicago stopped at the Illinois state line and on a clear day in Chicago you can see the result – the steel mills of Gary, Indiana, that can bring Dante's *Inferno* to mind. To the east of the mills lie the Indiana Dunes, over 15 miles of beaches and dunes formed by the prevailing winds off the lake.

This is Chicago's answer to the Hamptons, the one great bit of natural scenery in the whole region. It's one of the prime places for locals to go to the shore. You'll find long stretches of open beaches and dunes up to 100ft tall. You'll also find ponds, woodlands and nature walks. If you get bored you can stop at one of the Lake County casinos on your way home (see p. 98).

Most of the dunes are in the Indiana Dunes National Lakeshore or the Indiana Dunes State Park. There's a train service from the

## INFORMATION

*80 miles east of Chicago*

🚗 Dan Ryan Expwy (I-90) south to Chicago Skyway (I-90) past Hammond and Gary to join the I-94. Continue east on I-94 to the exit for Indiana Rte 249. Follow Rte 249 to US 12. Beaches and facilities are along US 12

☎ 219-926-7561

e www.nps.gov/indu

ⓘ West Beach Visitor Center (2 miles from intersection of US 12 and County Line Rd, 2 miles west of Ogden Dunes Station); Dorothy Buell Memorial Visitor Center (US 12 at Kemil Rd, 2 miles west of Beverly Shores station)

🕐 hours vary; call ☎ 219-926-7561

⑤ $4/carload, 50¢/person for walk-ins and cyclists, fee collected Memorial Day-Labor Day

✕ Brewster's Deli and Cafe (11 W Merchant St, New Buffalo; ☎ 616-469-3005)

Randolph St Station on the South Shore Line. Get off at the Ogden Dunes Station, the Dune Park Station or Beverly Shores.

# ORGANIZED TOURS

**Bus tours** run throughout the year. There are tours in big buses that offer a trip around town and tours on trolleys that let you hop on and off wherever you want. All suffer from the driver's commentaries, but that's a small price to pay for the convenience.

Most **boat tours** run from April to October, though some hardy souls do venture into the lake in the middle of winter. Some tours navigate the Chicago River, some run from the river into Lake Michigan and others run up and down the lakefront.

The best **walking tours** are the Chicago Architectural Foundation tours and the Chicago Neighborhood Tours run by the city's Office of Tourism.

**American Sightseeing** (5, L6) Two 2hr tours of town in big comfy buses. The North Tour runs from The Loop to Wrigley Field. The South Tour runs from Grant Park to Hyde Park. ✉ **55 E Monroe Dr, The Loop** ☎ **312-251-3100** ⏱ 10am (North Tour), noon (South Tour), 2pm (North Tour) ⑤ **$17/8.50 or $27/13.50 for both (cash only)**

**Chicago Trolley Company Tours** (5, L6) A 90min tour in motorized cable cars. Cars run every 15mins. Buy a day pass and get on and off as you wish. ✉ **Pick-up at stops including Art Institute, Sears Tower, Water Tower and Field Museum,** ☎ **312-663-0260** ⏱ 9am-5pm ⑤ **$18/15/8 (2-day ticket $20 adults)**

**Shoreline Sightseeing** (5, G10) A 30min narrated tour of the lakefront that runs from Navy Pier to Grant Park and back again ✉ **Navy Pier, Near North** ☎ **312-222-9328** ⏱ every 30mins from 11am-10pm ⑤ **$9/8/4**

**Chicago Neighborhood Tours** (5, K6) The best ticket in town. Four-hour tours of city neighborhoods by people who live there. See Bronzeville, Pilsen, Devon Ave and other places off the beaten track. ✉ **Chicago Cultural Center, The Loop** ☎ **312-742-1190** ⏱ **Sat 10am** ⑤ **$30/27**

**Bike Chicago** (5, G10) Free guided bike tours of Lincoln Park, Grant Park and the Japanese Gardens in Jackson Park. Or go it alone by simply checking the Web site. ✉ **Navy Pier; other locations at North Ave beach & 63rd St Beach, Near North** ☎ **312-755-0488** 🄴 **www.bike chicago.com** ⏱ April-Nov 11.30am & 1.30pm ⑤ bike rentals $7.75/hr, $30/day and up (kids $5/15)

## Transit Tours

Do your own city tour on a CTA bus. Watch how one neighborhood unfolds into the next as you roll down the street. Best bets include the No 22 up Clark St from The Loop to Andersonville (walk back over to the Red Line at Foster), the No 36 up State, Clark and Broadway from The Loop to Uptown (catch the Red Line anywhere from Sheridan to Berwyn) and the No 50 from the Damen stop on the Brown Line in Ravenswood to the Hoyne stop on the Blue Line two blocks west of the corner of Damen Ave and 20th St.

WELLS STREET

Richard I'Anson

**The Spirit of Chicago**
(5, G10) One of the lunch
and dinner cruises that run
from the south side of Navy
Pier unless the lake is frozen.
✉ Navy Pier, Near
North ☎ 312-836-7899
⏰ lunch cruises open
11-11.30am, leave dock
noon-12.30pm, return
2-2.30pm; dinner cruis-
es open 6-7pm, leave
dock 7-8pm, return 10-
11pm (call for details)
⑤ from $37.70 for
weekday lunch to
$97.73 for Sat dinner

**Wendella Sightseeing
Boats** (5, H6)
Choose from 1hr tours of
the river from the Michigan
Ave Bridge to the Sears
Tower or longer tours that
go into the lake and back.
✉ 400 N Michigan
Ave, Near North
☎ 312-337-1446
⏰ tours run Apr 15-
Oct 31 (weather per-
mitting); 90min tours
10am, 11.30am, 2pm,
3pm, 4.30pm, 7pm and
8.30pm; 1hr lake-only
tours 5.45pm; 2hr tours
Memorial Day-Labor
Day 7.30pm
⑤ $14/12/7 (cash only)

**Untouchable Tour**
(5, G4) The gangster tour
of the hit spots of the
1920s, from the site of the
St Valentine Day's Massacre
to the Biograph Theater
where Dellinger bought the
ranch. Book ahead.
✉ 600 N Clark St,
Near North
☎ 773-881-1195
⏰ Mon-Wed 10am;
Thurs 10am, 1pm; Fri
10am, 1pm, 7.30pm; Sat
10am, 1pm, 5pm; Sun
11am, 2pm ⑤ $20/15

## Chicago Architectural Foundation Tours

The CAF people will show you Chicago on foot or
bike, or by boat, bus or train.

Choose from a dozen different Loop walking
tours or the Loop train tours on Saturday that present Chicago from a new point of view two stories
above the sidewalk.

Take a river cruise from the **Mercury Cruise Line**
dock at Michigan Ave for yet another perspective on
the city. If you're able to plan ahead, book one of the
special tours, like a visit to Mies van der Rohe's glass
Farnsworth House.

**The Loop Tour Train** is free (bring your own fare
card). The walking tours generally cost $5-10. Call
☎ 312-922-8687 or check its website at
ⓔ www.architecture.org to consider all the options.

Peter Ptschelinzew

*Heading out on the water can save many a Chicago
visitor a bad case of a strained neck.*

# shopping

From the 1870s to the 1970s, the City of the Big Shoulders was the City of the Big Stores. Grand emporia lined State St from one end of The Loop to the other. Grandest of all was Marshall Field's, which covered a whole block on State and filled another building at Wabash and Washington Aves.

People met under the Field's clock at State and Washington or in the upstairs waiting rooms, ate in the Field's restaurants, and took away Frango mints from the Field's food halls.

The action crossed the river in the 1970s, as department stores died and racial tensions scared sub-urbanites and North Siders from The Loop. Field's opened a branch in the Water Tower complex and over the next 20 years vertical shop-ping malls appeared up and down Michigan Ave. The conversion of some State St stores into education-

*900 N Michigan Ave: shop 'til you drop.*

al campuses has brought students and life back into The Loop, but the Magnificent Mile on Michigan Ave remains the prime retail zone today.

## Shopping Districts

The other shopping districts are all on the North Side, except for Wicker Park/Bucktown in the Near Northwest, the home of the hip. Big-name boutiques (Prada, Escada and Barney's) line Oak St from Michigan Ave to Rush St. You'll find big names and no-names along Halsted St from North Ave to Fullerton. The stretch of Halsted from Belmont to Addison is Boystown, perfect for club clothes and rainbow-flag trinkets, while the strip of Belmont around Halsted and Clark is used-clothing central.

Broadway and Clark in Lincoln Park and Lakeview are nice neigh-borhood shopping streets for nice-upper-middle class neighborhoods. Consumers from every part of the North Side crowd the new Sheffield-North Commons near North and Clybourn Aves to fill Volvo wagons with groceries, liquors or coffee.

### 24 Hours

For a place that goes to bed early, Chicago has lots of choices if you need ice cream, a magazine, some smokes or some aspirin at 4am. There are a half-dozen 24hr **Walgreen's** on the North Side alone, including at 757 N Michigan Ave at Chicago Ave (5, F6; ☎ 312-664-4000) and 3201 N Broadway at Belmont Ave (4, C3; ☎ 773-327-3308) with pharmacies open 24-7 as well. The newsstand in front of Walgreen's on N Michigan Ave is also open 24-7. Most of the Jewel and Dominick's supermar-kets on the North Side are open 24hr, including the Jewel at 3531 N Broadway (4, B3; ☎ 773-871-1054) and the Dominick's at 424 W Division St (5, C4; ☎ 312-274-1299).

# DEPARTMENT STORES

### Bloomingdale's (5, E6)

You can find branches of New York's best-known department store in lots of cities outside New York these days, but somehow the Bloomingdale's people manage to maintain their edge, with an exceptional selection of clothes and accessories from the big-name designers, from the new-name designers and from their own private-label operations.

✉ **900 N Michigan Ave, Near North**
☎ **312-440-4460**
🚇 **Chicago (Red)**
🚌 **3, 145, 146, 147, 151**
🕐 **Mon-Sat 10am-8pm, Sun 11am-6pm**

### Filene's Basement

**(5, F6)** You might find a real deal among the men's and women's clothes and accessories in this discount operation. Then again, you might not. Nothing ventured, nothing gained.

✉ **830 N Michigan Ave, Near North**
☎ **312-482-8918**
🚇 **Chicago (Red)**
🚌 **3, 145, 146, 147, 151** 🕐 **Mon-Fri 10am-9pm, Sat 10am-8pm, Sun 11am-7pm**

### Marshall Field's (5, K5)

More than 100 years after Marshall Field told his clerks that 'the customer is always right', the flagship of the Field's chain remains one of the world's great department stores. Wander the grand ground-floor arcades, explore the children's world or eat in the Walnut Room or the food court on the 7th floor.

✉ **111 N State St, The Loop** ☎ **312-781-1000**
🚇 **Washington**
🚋 **Randolph**
🚌 **6, 29, 36, 62, 146**
🕐 **Mon-Sat 10am-7pm, Sun 11am-6pm**

### Nieman-Marcus (5, F6)

You don't need big hair to shop in this branch of the great Texas emporium, but you will need cash or an American Express card, because they don't take anything else. Top-flight style, top-flight service, top-flight prices (you get what you pay for).

✉ **737 N Michigan Ave, Near North**
☎ **312-642-5900**
🚇 **Chicago (Red)**
🚌 **3, 145, 146, 147, 151**
🕐 **Mon-Sat 10am-7pm, Sun noon-6pm**

*Marshall Field's has stood the test of time.*

### Nordstrom (5, G6)

Nordstrom started as a shoe store in Seattle and shoppers still come for the shoe selection and shoe-store level of personal service. A lot of substance, and not a lot of flash.

✉ **55 E Grand Ave at Wabash Ave, Near North** ☎ **312-464-1515**
🚇 **Grand** 🚌 **3, 145, 146, 147, 151, 157**
🕐 **Mon-Thurs 10am-8pm, Fri & Sat 10am-9pm, Sun 11am-7pm**

### Saks Fifth Ave (5, F6)

The grand dame of Fifth Ave has been a grand dame on Michigan Ave for decades. Top-end lines for men and women. Few surprises but few disappointments, either.

✉ **Chicago Place, 700 N Michigan Ave, Near North** ☎ **312-944-6500**
🚇 **Chicago (Red)**
🚌 **3, 145, 146, 147, 151**
🕐 **Mon-Sat 10am-7pm, Sun noon-6pm**

*Bloomingdale's in full bloom*

# MARKETS & MALLS

Because the weather's so rough, there's only one full-time outdoor market in Chicago and only a few seasonal farmer's markets – best bets are Tuesday at the Federal Center Plaza (5, L5) and Thursday at the Daley Center Plaza (5, K5) from June to October. You'll find vertical marketplaces instead, in old buildings in The Loop and in new malls on Michigan Ave.

### Jeweler's Building
(5, K6) You could spend days shopping here, working your way from one floor to the next, looking for that perfect stone or that perfect bargain. Not for the faint-hearted (you should have some idea about what you're looking for before you start or the choices will kill you). ⊠ 5 S Wabash Ave, The Loop ☎ 312-853-2057 ⊕ Madison, Washington 🚌 3, 4, 6, 29, 36, 62, 146, 151 ⏲ Mon-Fri 8am-6pm, Sat 8am-5.30pm

### Maxwell St Market
(5, P3) A century ago, Maxwell St was the heart of Chicago's Jewish ghetto. The poor immigrant Jews and their pushcarts are long gone and Maxwell St itself is gone, too, bulldozed by University of Illinois at Chicago. The relocated market serves the new immigrants in town. Look for tamale stands amid the piles of T-shirts and spare auto parts. ⊠ S Canal St at W Roosevelt, Near West Side ☎ 312-922-3100 ⊕ Roosevelt (Red) 🚌 12 ⏲ 7am-3pm

### Music Mart at DePaul Center (5, M5)
A collection of fine music shops occupies the lower floors of DePaul University's downtown campus. Free concerts most weekdays at lunchtime. ⊠ 333 S State St, The Loop ☎ 312-362-6700 ⊕ Jackson, Library 🚌 36, 145, 146, 147, 151 ⏲ vary by store

### 900 N Michigan (5, E6)
The biggest, the chicest, the most gracious of the malls along Michigan Ave. Start with Bloomingdale's as an anchor tenant, add dozens of upscale boutiques, top it off with condominiums and a Four Seasons Hotel, simmer in a few years of experience and you have the best indoor shopping experience in town this side of Field's at Christmas. ⊠ 900 N Michigan Ave, Near North ☎ 312-915-3916 ⊕ Chicago (Red) 🚌 3, 145, 146, 147, 151 ⏲ Mon-Sat 10am-7pm, Sun noon-6pm

*Bloomingdale's not your style? Head to Maxwell St Market*

*The Shops at North Bridge*

### The Shops at North Bridge (5, G6)

The newest entry in the Magnificent Mile sweepstakes is a mix of conventional mall stores and the unconventional. The entire 3rd floor is dedicated to children's stores. The 4th is set aside for food, including a cafe from the owner of Tuscany and hot dogs from the folks at Fluky's.

✉ **520 N Michigan Ave, Near North**
☎ **312-327-2300**
🅾 **Chicago (Red)**
🚌 **3, 145, 146, 147, 151**
🕐 **Mon-Sat 10am-8pm, Sun 11am-6pm**

### Water Tower Place (5, E6)

The first mall to bring suburban comforts to the Magnificent Mile, Water Tower Place has over 100 stores on eight levels, anchored by Field's and Lord & Taylor on the ground floor. It also has two cinemas, a food court, upscale apartments and the Ritz-Carlton Hotel. Who cares if it's snowing outside?

✉ **835 N Michigan Ave, Near North**
☎ **312-440-3166**
🅾 **Chicago (Red)**
🚌 **3, 145, 146, 147, 151**
🕐 **Mon-Thurs 10am-7pm, Fri 10am-6pm, Sun noon-6pm**

### Woodfield Mall (1, C1)

Woodfield is still considered the largest mall in the world (other malls might be bigger, but none have as much retail space). If you're out in the northwest suburbs and you need something – anything – you are likely to find it here. Just remember where you parked.

✉ **Hwy 53 at Woodfield Rd, Schaumburg**
☎ **847-330-1537**
🚗 **Kennedy Expwy (I-90) from city, past O'Hare airport to Hwy 53 interchange, south on Hwy 53 to Woodfield Rd**
🕐 **Mon-Sat 10am-9pm, Sun 11am-6pm**

*Water Tower Place: not a place to throw stones.*

## CLOTHING & JEWELRY

### Alternatives (5, E5)

Men's and women's shoes for 20-somethings and shoe buyers who think like 20-somethings at prices that 20-somethings can afford. Also in Old Town at 1969 N Halsted St.

✉ **942 N Rush St, Near North** ☎ **312-266-1545**
🅾 **Chicago (Red)**
🚌 **145, 146, 147, 151**
🕐 **Mon-Sat 10am-7pm, Sun noon-6pm**

### Barney's (5, D5)

Not grandiose like the big Barney's stores in NYC or LA, but still pretty grand. Shop for Barney's own private labels or its first-rate selection of shoes. Perfect for PIBs (people-in-black).

✉ **25 E Oak St, Gold Coast** ☎ **312-587-1700**
🅾 **Chicago (Red)**
🚌 **3, 145, 146, 147, 151**
🕐 **Mon-Sat 10am-7pm, Sun noon-6pm**

### June Blaker (5, F4)

The clothes and accessories for both men and women here are in perfect tune with its location in the middle of the River North galleries. Not everything on the racks is black but almost everything has a real edge.

✉ **200 W Superior St, River North** ☎ **312-751-9220** 🅾 **Chicago (Brown)** 🚌 **66, 156**
🕐 **Mon-Sat 10am-6pm**

**Body Body Wear**
(4, C3) Truth in advertising in the window. These well-made men's clothes by Toronto designer Stephen Sandler show off your body whether you want to or not. Not a good place to shop after a big heavy lunch.
✉ 3259 N Broadway, Lakeview ☎ 773-388-0277 Ⓜ Belmont
🚌 36, 77, 156
🕐 Mon-Thurs noon-8pm, Fri & Sat noon-9pm, Sun noon-6pm

**Bombshell** (4, C2)
Young women's clothes for those who are serious clotheshorses or young women just looking for something a little special. From the owners of Tragically Hip next door at 931 W Belmont Ave.
✉ 933 W Belmont Ave, Lakeview ☎ 773-244-4201 Ⓜ Belmont
🚌 8, 22, 77
🕐 Mon-Sat 11am-7pm, Sun 11am-6pm

**Donald J Pliner** (5, D6)
Striking shoes for men and women beautifully made in the mountains of Italy, as it says on the insoles. Prada league gear without Prada attitude, at one of only two Pliner boutiques in the US.
✉ 106 E Oak St, Gold Coast ☎ 312-202-9600

Ⓜ Chicago (Red)
🚌 3, 145, 146, 147, 151
🕐 Mon-Sat 10am-6pm, Sun 11am-5pm

**Linda Campisano Millinery** (5, E6)
Yes, a Windy City hat store, with classy men's hats and flights of fancy for women. Also known for custom-made bridal veils and headpieces.
✉ 900 N Michigan Ave, Near North
☎ 312-337-1004
Ⓜ Grand (Red)
🚌 3, 45, 146, 147, 151
🕐 Mon-Sat 10am-7pm, Sun noon-6pm

**Mosaic** (4, F3)
'My Own Store on Armitage in Chicago' carries trendy, elegant sportswear for women who are young and slim and rich. Great clothes for girls and

great girl-watching for guys who go for Darryl Hannah lookalikes.
✉ 843 W Armitage Ave, Old Town ☎ 312-935-1131 Ⓜ Armitage
🚌 8, 73 🕐 Mon-Fri 10am-7pm, Sat 10am-6pm, Sun noon-5pm

**Mark Shale** (5, E6)
Men's and women's clothes with their own sense of style, a mix of private-label and international labels that you won't see in every mall across America. Worth a detour on any expedition to the Magnificent Mile.
✉ 900 N Michigan Ave, Near North
☎ 312-440-0720
Ⓜ Chicago (Red)
🚌 3, 145, 146, 147, 151
🕐 Mon-Thurs 10am-7pm, Fri 10am-8pm, Sat 10am-6pm, Sun noon-6pm

---

## The Usual Suspects
Although the main shopping streets of the North Side are remarkably free from national chain store logos (save the omnipresent Walgreen's and Starbucks), you can find all of the national chains in the vertical malls on Michigan Ave. If you only have time for one mall, make it Water Tower Place, which has **Gap**, **Gap Kids**, **Banana Republic**, **The Limited**, **Sharper Image** and **Abercrombie & Fitch** among many, many others.

---

## Secondhand Stores
Belmont Ave is to vintage clothes what Oak St is to top-end European designers. **Hollywood Mirror** (4, C3; 812 W Belmont Ave, ☎ 773-404-4510) and its neighbor **Ragstock** (upstairs, enter from the alley on the west side of the building, ☎ 773-868-9263) have racks of used clothes, along with new clothes to match that used-clothes look. **Silver Moon**, around the corner at 3337 N Halsted St (4, C3; ☎ 773-883-0222), has jackets and suits and vintage wedding dresses. If you're still not satisfied, head up to **Flashy Trash** (4, B3; 3524 N Halsted St, ☎ 773-327-6900), where that perfect leisure suit or gangster hat may be waiting.

# ANTIQUES & FURNITURE

### Antiques Centre at Kinzie Sq (5, H4)

One of the high-end antiques warehouses in the River North area, with dealers featuring furniture, ceramics, silver and more, mainly European and American, dating from the 1700s to the 1900s.

✉ 220 W Kinzie St, River North
☎ 312-464-1946
🚇 Merchandise Mart
🚌 156
🕐 Mon-Fri 10am-5pm, Sat noon-4pm

### Asian House of Chicago (5, H4)

Asian furniture and furnishings from very large Japanese tonsu and Chinese elmwood chests to decorative objects you can slip into your suitcase.

✉ 159 W Kinzie St, River North ☎ 312-527-4848 🚇 Merchandise Mart 🚌 156
🕐 Mon-Sat 10am-6pm

### Broadway Antique Market (3, A7)

A true indoor marketplace of over 20,000 sq ft with 75 different dealers selling anything from the Victorian to mid-century modern. If you're looking for something in particular, just ask the managers and they'll give you some tips.

✉ 6130 N Broadway, Uptown ☎ 773-868-0285 🚇 Granville
🚌 36 🕐 Mon-Sat 11am-7pm, Sun noon-6pm

### Crate & Barrel (5, E6)

About 30 years ago, Crate & Barrel started selling modish but modest china and kitchen stuff out of crates and barrels in a storefront in Old Town. Now it sells modish but modest china, kitchen stuff, furniture and furnishings from coast to coast. This is the flagship store, an exercise in consistent good taste from outside to in.

✉ 646 N Michigan Ave, Near North
☎ 312-787-5900
🚇 Grand 🚌 3, 145, 146, 147, 151, 157
🕐 Mon-Fri 10am-7pm, Sat 10am-6pm, Sun 11am-6pm

### Golden Triangle (5, H4)

Saffron silk throw pillows, 19th-century opium beds and other high-end furniture, textiles and art objects from East and Southeast Asia in a handsome River North space.

✉ 72 W Hubbard St, River North
☎ 312-755-1266
🚇 Merchandise Mart, Grand 🚌 65, 156
🕐 Mon-Fri 10am-7pm, Sat 10am-5pm

### Material Culture (5, H4)

One of those places where people do well by doing good. Fine contemporary Oriental carpets from Turkey, India and China made in traditional ways with natural dyes, all very easy on the eyes, with an assortment of furniture and odds and ends that would make William Morris proud.

✉ 401 N LaSalle St, River North
☎ 312-467-1490
🚇 Merchandise Mart, Grand 🚌 65, 156
🕐 Mon-Fri 10am-6pm, Sat 10am-5pm, Sun noon-5pm

### Jay Robert's Antiques Warehouse (5, H4)

A big barn of a place in River North, filled mainly with 19th- and early 20th-century stuff that underscores the loose meaning of 'antique' in American English while it piques the curiosity of the shopper. Go for it.

✉ 149 W Kinzie St, River North
☎ 312-222-0167
🚇 Merchandise Mart
🚌 156
🕐 Mon-Sat 10am-5pm

### Salvage One (3, E7)

A five-floor warehouse filled with furniture and architectural fixtures. Worth a trip to the West Side if you're looking for claw foot tubs, mantelpieces or other bits to restore your abode.

✉ 1524 S Sangamon St, Pilsen ☎ 312-733-0098 🚉 Halsted 🚌 8
🕐 Mon-Sat 10am-5pm, Sun 11am-4pm

*Cultural material*

# MUSIC & BOOKS

**Act I Bookstore** (4, E3)
The resource center for the Chicago theater scene. Find a copy of the script from an old Neil Simon play, a copy of the latest edition of Variety or an esoteric tract on The Method or theater design.
✉ **2450 N Lincoln Ave, Lincoln Park** ☎ **773-348-6757** Ⓜ **Fullerton** 🚍 **8, 11** ⏰ **Mon-Fri 10am-8pm, Sat 10am-6pm, Sun noon-6pm**

**Afrocentric Book Store** (5, M5)
One of the largest collections of materials on African and African American culture in the country, let alone the city, in a convenient location in the DePaul University center downtown.
✉ **333 S State St, The Loop** ☎ **312-939-1956** Ⓜ **Jackson** 🚍 **145, 146, 147, 151** ⏰ **Mon-Fri 9.30am-6pm, Sat 10am-4.30pm**

**Barbara's Bookstore** (5, B4) A locally owned bookstore that has branches all over town, like so many other local book-stores and restaurants. The Old Town branch is large and cozy at the same time.
✉ **1350 N Wells St, Old Town** ☎ **312-642-5044** Ⓜ **Clark/Division** 🚍 **156** ⏰ **Mon-Sat 9am-10pm, Sun 10am-9pm**

**Chicago Comics** (4, C3)
The place to find R Crumb, the Fabulous Furry Freak brothers or their contemporary counterparts on the North Side. Who knows, the staff might even give you a hand if you're not sure what you're looking for.
✉ **3244 N Clark St, Lakeview** ☎ **773-528-1983** Ⓜ **Belmont** 🚍 **8, 22, 77** ⏰ **Mon-Fri noon-8pm, Sat 11am-8pm, Sun noon-6pm**

**Evil Clown** (4, B3)
Best indie record shop on the North Side, featuring new and used CDs (no vinyl, please) that you can listen to before you commit.
✉ **3418 N Halsted St, Wrigleyville** ☎ **773-472-4761** Ⓜ **Addison** 🚍 **8, 36** ⏰ **Mon-Fri noon-10pm, Sat noon-9pm, Sun noon-7pm**

**Europa Books** (5, E5)
The best foreign-language bookstore in town, carrying books and magazines in European languages including French, German, Spanish, Italian, Portuguese and Russian.
✉ **832 N State St, Near North** ☎ **312-335-9677** Ⓜ **Chicago (Red)** 🚍 **36** ⏰ **Mon-Fri 8am-8pm, Sat 9am-8pm, Sun 9am-6pm**

**Jazz Record Mart** (5, G5) Here, they claim to have the largest collection of jazz and blues in the world and when you walk down the aisles you suspect that they're right. Related fields of gospel, world music and R & B are represented as well.
✉ **444 N Wabash Ave, Near North** ☎ **312-222-1467** Ⓜ **Grand** 🚍 **36, 65** ⏰ **Mon-Sat 10am-8pm, Sun noon-5pm**

**Powell's North** (4, D2)
One of three Powell's locations that offer a mix of new and used books. Powell's North has the best art and architecture sections and the largest rare-book room. Powell's South in Hyde Park (7, D6; 1501 E 57th St) is more scholastically minded.
✉ **2850 N Lincoln Ave, Lincoln Park** ☎ **773-248-1444** Ⓜ **Diversey** 🚍 **8, 11, 74** ⏰ **Sun-Fri 11am-9pm, Sat 10am-10pm**

**Prairie Avenue Book Store** (5, M6)
An architectural gem of an architecture/design

*Want to bring the blues back home?*

Richard Cummins

## Books on Chicago

Chicago has been a subject and a base for writers since the city exploded before the turn of the 20th century. There are books about Chicago, books set in Chicago and books informed by Chicago life.

In the first category, *Nature's Metropolis* by William Cronin is an extraordinary natural history of the city. *Boss* by the late newspaperman Mike Royko is a vivid portrait of the first Mayor Daley. In the second category, *The Jungle* by Upton Sinclair exposed the world of the stockyards, while Nelson Algren's *The Man with the Golden Arm* and Theodore Dresier's *Sister Carrie* exposed the harsh realities of life elsewhere in town. The city is almost another character in contemporary murder mysteries by Sara Paretsky *(VI Warshawski)* and Scott Turow *(Presumed Innocent)*.

In the third category, almost everything by Studs Terkel, including his masterpiece *Working* and Saul Bellow, including his masterpiece *Henderson the Rain King*, has the sound of a conversation overheard on the El.

---

bookstore, with over 12,000 books on design from the general (picture books on architecture or furniture) to the esoteric (codes and manuals and project management). Ideal for browsing or serious research.
✉ 418 S Wabash Ave, The Loop ☎ 312-922-8311 Ⓙ Jackson, Library 🚌 145, 146, 147, 151 ⏰ Mon-Fri 10am-6pm, Sat 10am-4pm

### Quimby's (2, D4)

The best 'zine stand in town, filled with underground comics, independent magazines and the truly strange. If you can get it on your neighborhood newsstand, don't look for it here.
✉ 1854 W North Ave, Wicker Park
☎ 773-342-0910
Ⓙ Damen 🚌 72, 50, 56 ⏰ Mon-Thurs noon-8pm, Fri & Sat noon-10pm, Sun noon-6pm

### Reckless Records

(2, D4) A record shop straight from Nick Hornsby's *High Fidelity*. Physically untidy and intellectually vibrant. Hustle on over, maybe strike up a conversation with a clerk, and see for yourself.
✉ 1532 Milwaukee Ave, Wicker Park
☎ 773-235-3727
Ⓙ Damen 🚌 50, 56, 72 ⏰ Mon-Sat 10am-10pm, Sun 10am-8pm

### The Savvy Traveler

(5, M6) This may be the best travel bookstore in the US. Even its location, in a Chicago Style classic on Michigan Ave, is a call to the open road. A great assortment of travel gadgets to complement the guides and maps and memoirs. If you can't find it here, it may not exist.
✉ 310 S Michigan Ave, The Loop ☎ 312-913-9800 Ⓙ Adams,

Jackson 🚌 3, 6, 151
⏰ Mon-Sat 10am-7.30pm, Sun noon-5pm

### Tower Records (4, E4)

Tower may be the best of the chain music stores. Not as chic as Virgin perhaps, but both the North Clark store and the sister store in the Loop at 214 S Wabash Ave house astonishing assortments from pop to classical to jazz to world, with videos, books and magazines to boot if you need some other sensory input.
✉ 2301 N Clark St, Lincoln Park
☎ 773-477-5994
Ⓙ Fullerton 🚌 22
⏰ 9am-midnight (Ticketmaster to 8.30pm)

### Unabridged Bookstore (4, C3)

The best neighborhood bookstore in Lakeview, with something for everyone in the neighborhood. A large children's section, a large travel section, a large gay & lesbian section and lots and lots of magazines.
✉ 3251 N Broadway, Lakeview ☎ 773-883-9119 Ⓙ Belmont
🚌 36, 77, 151
⏰ Mon-Fri 10am-10pm, Sat & Sun 10am-8pm

### Women & Children First (3, B7)

A feminist bookstore in the heart of Andersonville that also stocks children's books and a range of music and videos and posters that work with its message.
✉ 5233 N Clark St, Andersonville ☎ 773-769-9299 Ⓙ Berwyn
🚌 22 ⏰ Mon & Tues 11am-7pm, Wed-Fri 11am-9pm, Sat 10am-7pm, Sun 11am-6pm

# ARTS & CRAFTS

**ArtEffect** (4, F4)
Crossing all kinds of lines, ArtEffect has almost any kind of gift for a woman from handcrafted objects to handcrafted clothing and furniture that underscore the 'art' in its name.
✉ **651 W Armitage Ave, Old Town** ☎ **312-664-0997** 🚇 **Sedgwick** 🚌 **11, 22, 36, 73**
🕐 Mon-Thurs 11am-7pm, Fri 11am-6pm, Sat 10am-6pm, Sun noon-5pm

**Greens, Inc** (4, F4)
A wondrous clutter of ethnographic objects, such as Balinese temple carvings, beaded masks, and feathered New Guinea headdresses, peek out among masses of orchids and other exotic flowers and cactuses. Slow down and smell 'dem roses.
✉ **1718 N Wells St, Old Town** ☎ **312-266-2806** 🚇 **Sedgwick** 🚌 **72, 156**
🕐 Mon-Sat 9am-7pm, Sun 11am-6pm

**Illinois Artisans Shop** (5, J4) Twice a year, a jury for the Illinois Department of Natural Resources selects work from Illinois artisans to sell here in the Thompson Center downtown.
✉ **James R Thompson Center, 100 W Randolph St, The Loop** ☎ **312-814-5321** 🚇 **Clark** 🚌 **22, 156**
🕐 Mon-Fri 9am-5pm

**Northern Possessions** (5, E6) One-of-a-kind pieces from over 1200 North American artisans. Clothing, jewelry and wearable art like vintage bakelite purses, displayed beautifully in a shop in the mall with the Bloomingdale's.
✉ **900 N Michigan Ave, Near North** ☎ **312-397-0300** 🚇 **Chicago (Red)** 🚌 **3, 145, 146, 147, 151**
🕐 Mon-Sat 10am-7pm, Sun noon-6pm

**Portia** (5, F3)
A River North gallery devoted entirely to works in glass. Some are small, leaning toward the 'craft' in 'arts & crafts,' others are large, leaning towards the 'art' side. Particularly nice to visit on a gloomy day.
✉ **207 W Superior St, River North** ☎ **312-932-9500** 🚇 **Chicago (Brown)** 🚌 **156**
🕐 Tues-Sat 11am-5pm

*Local artsists are given a head start via community projects such as Gallery 37.*

# FOOD & DRINK

**Breadsmith** (4, F4)
Handmade European breads baked on the premises in a special eight-ton steam injection stone hearth oven. Try standards like the French peasant or the ciabatta or one of the daily specials like maple raisin walnut and honey oat (available Mondays) or traditional rye and challah (available Friday, of course).
✉ **1710 N Wells St,** Old Town
☎ **312-642-5858** 🚇 **Sedgwick** 🚌 **72, 156**
🕐 7.30am-7.30pm

**Chalet on the Gold Coast** (5, E5)
Calling Chalet a wine & cheese shop is like calling Cartier a rock shop. This place has an astute selection of wines from everywhere in every price range, with cheeses and charcuterie that could hold their own in France.
✉ **40 E Delaware Pl, Near North**
☎ **312-787-8555** 🚇 **Chicago (Red)** 🚌 **36, 145, 146, 147, 151** 🕐 **Mon-Thurs & Sat 10am-8pm, Fri 10am-9pm, Sun 10am-6pm**

**Paulina Market** (4, B1)
One of the largest selections of sausages you'll find in a

city that knows and loves its sausages. German? Italian? Polish? They've got them. Want something more exotic, like a venison medallion or an ostrich steak? Just ask. ✉ **3501 N Lincoln Ave, Lakeview West** ☎ **773-248-6272** Ⓜ **Paulina, Addison (Brown)** 🚌 **22, 152** ⏱ **Mon-Wed & Fri 9am-6pm, Thurs 9am-7pm, Sat 9am-5pm**

### Peets Coffee (4, G2)

The people from Berkeley who taught the Starbucks people about coffee have opened in the Sheffield-North Commons, which is rapidly becoming the Gourmet Ghetto of the North Side. Come taste the difference for yourself. ✉ **1000 W North Ave, Old Town** ☎ **312-475-9782** Ⓜ **North/Clybourn** 🚌 **8, 72** ⏱ **Mon-Fri 8am-6pm, Sat 7am-8pm, Sun 8am-7pm**

### Red Hen Bread (2, D3)

The best – some say the only – French bread in town comes from this Wicker Park hole-in-the-wall. Other kinds of breads, too, and cookies and pastries to take home for a secret snack. ✉ **1623 N Milwaukee Ave, Wicker Park/Bucktown** ☎ **773-342-6823** Ⓜ **Damen** 🚌 **72, 50, 56** ⏱ **Mon-Sat 7.30am-7.30pm, Sun 9am-5pm**

### Sam's Wines & Spirits

(4, F2) A warehouse-club operation in Sheffield-North Commons near Peets. A range of wines from just about every wine-producing area in the world, at just about every price point you could ask for. ✉ **1720 N Marcey St,**

### Old Town

☎ **312-664-4394** Ⓜ **North/Clybourn** 🚌 **8, 72** ⏱ **Mon-Sat 8am-9pm, Sun 11am-6pm**

*Swede tooth*

### The Swedish Bakery

(3, B7) Traditional Swedish pastries like marzariner (almond tarts), toska tortes and strudels share the spotlight with coffee cakes, cookies, sweet rolls and classic European goods like mocha logs, eclairs and Napoleons. A good place for dentists. A bad place for diets. ✉ **5348 N Clark St, Andersonville** ☎ **773-561-8919** Ⓜ **Berwyn** 🚌 **22** ⏱ **Mon-Thurs 6.30am-6.30pm, Fri 6.30am-8pm, Sat 6.30am-5pm**

### Sweet Mysteries Bakery (4, C1)

Spectacular cookies and pastries including moist, chewy ruggeleh better than almost anyone's grandma ever made. If you have blood-sugar problems consider some of the savory snacks and sandwiches also available. ✉ **3335 N Southport Ave, Lakeview West** ☎ **773-404-2900** Ⓜ **Southport** ⏱ **Tues-Fri 8.30am-7.30pm, Sat 9.30am-6pm**

### Wikstrom's Delicatessen (3, B7)

The kind of place that put the 'Anderson' into 'Andersonville.' Pick up some potato lefsa, herring or Swedish meatballs. Who knows, you may have to take a hot dish somewhere. Or order a sandwich to go and enjoy the neighborhood. ✉ **5427 N Clark St, Andersonville** ☎ **773-275-6100** Ⓜ **Berwyn** 🚌 **22** ⏱ **Mon-Sat 9am-6pm, Sun 11am-4pm**

### Whole Foods (4, G2)

Those hippies from Austin, Texas have invaded Chicagoland, and the yuppies from Lincoln Park and vicinity have surrendered to the lure of good produce, great meats, fabulous delicatessen and sensational service. Avoid the parking lot on the weekends if you can. ✉ **1000 W North Ave, Old Town** ☎ **773-587-0648** Ⓜ **North/Clybourn** 🚌 **9, 72** ⏱ **8am-10pm**

### Vosges Haut Chocolates (5, G6)

Stunning truffles in edgy flavors like Naga (milk chocolate and coconut with a sprinkling of curry) and Red Fire (dark chocolate with cinnamon and a touch of red chilli). Couture cocoa powders for those cold winter nights. Five kinds of chocolate bars. All wrapped in the best packaging on the whole Mag Mile. ✉ **Shops at North Bridge, 520 N Michigan Ave, Near North** ☎ **773-772-5349** Ⓜ **Grand** 🚌 **3, 145, 146, 147, 151, 157** ⏱ **Mon-Sat 10am-8pm, Sun 11am-6pm**

# SHOPPING FOR CHILDREN

**American Girl Place**
(5, F6) Where Eloise went shopping when she left home. Three floors of precious things for girls and their dolls, including a cafe that serves lunch, dinner and teas. The American Girls Revue plays Thursday through Sunday (phone for details).
✉ **111 E Chicago Ave, Near North** ☎ **312-255-9876** Ⓗ **Chicago (Red)** 🚍 **3, 66, 145, 146, 147, 151** ⊘ **Mon-Wed & Sun 10am-7pm, Thurs-Sat 10am-9pm**

**Cella for Baby** (4, E3)
A boutique for babies, featuring clothes and infant gear appropriate to its location amid the more adult boutiques of Lincoln Park. A welcome relief from the chain stores.
✉ **2310 N Lincoln Ave, Lincoln Park** ☎ **773-472-9380** Ⓗ **Fullerton** 🚍 **8, 11, 74** ⊘ **Tues-Sat 10am-5pm, Sun 11am-5pm**

**Children in Paradise Books** (5, E5)
A dreamy space in the middle of the Near North shopping mania. Pull up a chair in the reading corner and give yourself or a small traveling companion time out for a little story. The staff will help you find something appropriate for a special age group.
✉ **909 N Rush St, Near North** ☎ **312-951-5437** Ⓗ **Grand (Red)** 🚍 **145, 146, 147, 151** ⊘ **Mon-Thurs 10am-7pm, Fri 10am-8pm, Sat & Sun noon-5pm**

**Saturday's Child** (4, E3)
The anti-Toys R Us, a boutique toy store with an emphasis on toys that engage the mind and don't need batteries.
✉ **2146 N Halsted St, Lincoln Park** ☎ **773-525-8697** Ⓗ **Fullerton** 🚍 **8, 74** ⊘ **Mon-Thurs & Sat 10am-6pm, Fri 10am-7pm, Sun 11am-5pm**

**FAO Schwarz** (5, E6)
The brand name in fancy toy stores, and for a very good reason. Lots of different kinds of toys and games in a space that's fun to be in (except perhaps at holiday time).
✉ **840 N Michigan Ave, Near North** ☎ **312-587-5000** Ⓗ **Chicago (Red)** 🚍 **145, 146, 147, 151** ⊘ **10am-6pm**

**Second Child** (4, F3)
Ever wonder where the $200 baby dress goes when baby grows out of it? Some of the fanciest baby clothes a grandmother could buy end up here, at this toney resale shop for children's clothes.
✉ **954 W Armitage Ave, Old Town** ☎ **773-883-0840** Ⓗ **Armitage** 🚍 **8, 73** ⊘ **Mon-Sat 10am-6pm, Sun noon-5pm**

**Target** (3, C7)
Style-conscious, cost-conscious parents and grandparents flocked to Target for some of the best buys in children's clothes long before the Target folks started turning out toasters for yuppies. Look for other with-it gear at bargain prices while you're there.
✉ **2656 N Elston Ave, North Side** ☎ **773-252-1994** 🚍 **49, 74, 76** ⊘ **8am-10pm**

**Toys R Us** (5, L5)
You'll find the convenience of a suburban big-box toy store right here in The Loop. Not for the faint-hearted at holiday time.
✉ **10 S State St, The Loop** ☎ **312-857-0667** Ⓗ **Madison, Monroe** 🚍 **145, 146, 147, 151** ⊘ **Mon-Sat 9.30am-7pm (Thurs to 8pm), Sun noon-7pm**

*Jumping moons is udder fun on the Mag Mile.*

Richard Cummins

# SPECIALIST STUFF

### Best Buy (4, G3)
All kinds of gadgets and devices from TVs and DVD players to cameras, printers and MP3 players. It carries software as well as hardware, CDs, DVDs and games among other things. All on the edge of the Old Town in the consumer haven of Sheffield-North Commons.
✉ **1000 W North Ave, Old Town** ☎ **312-988-4067** Ⓣ **North/Clybourn** 🚌 **8, 72** ⏰ **Mon-Sat 10am-9pm, Sun 11am-6pm**

### Central Camera (5, L6)
A store for professionals and camera buffs who want to be treated like professionals. Everything from special lenses or film to standard film processing competently done (ask about the student and teacher discounts on processing ).
✉ **230 S Wabash Ave, The Loop** ☎ **312-427-5580** Ⓣ **Adams, Jackson** 🚌 **36, 145, 146, 147, 151** ⏰ **Mon-Fri 8.30am-5.30pm, Sat 8.30am-5pm**

### Jazz Baby (4, C2)
A store dedicated to the swing era. Clothing, shoes and jewelry to go out for a night doing West Coast Swing and the Lindy, with other objects that look right at home alongside a saxophone.
✉ **3228 N Clark St, Lakeview** ☎ **773-935-8323** Ⓣ **Belmont** 🚌 **8, 22, 77** ⏰ **noon-8pm**

### Paper Source (5, E3)
Paper in any shape, size, color and texture for every purpose you can imagine, along with rubber stamps and ribbon and other complementary items. If can't

---

**Tax Tips**
Illinois charges 2% sales tax on food and 8.75% on almost everything else. If you're from out of state (or out of the country) and the store you're shopping in does not have a branch back home, you can generally avoid sales tax by having your purchases shipped directly home. At these rates, it may be worth it.

---

find what you're looking for here, have a look in **Pearl Art Supply** across the street.
✉ **232 W Chicago Ave, River North** ☎ **312-915-0200** Ⓣ **Chicago (Brown)** 🚌 **66, 156** ⏰ **Mon-Sat 9am-7pm, Sun noon-5pm**

### Sportmart (5, G4)
Eight full floors of gear for every sport you can imagine (with the possible exceptions of curling and ice fishing). Memorabilia from local sports icons decorate the store and draw crowds of visitors during the summer and the holidays. Also in Lakeview at 3134 N Clark St.
✉ **620 N LaSalle St, River North** ☎ **312-337-6151** Ⓣ **Chicago (Brown, Red)** 🚌 **156** ⏰ **Mon-Fri 9.30am-9.30pm, Sat 9am-9pm, Sun 10am-7pm**

### Village Cycle Center (5, B4)
The largest bike store in the nation carries Trek, Specialized and Klein bikes and an overwhelming assortment of accessories for bikes and cyclists.
✉ **1337 N Wells St, Old Town** ☎ **312-751-2488** Ⓣ **Clark/Division, Sedgwick** 🚌 **156** ⏰ **Mon-Fri 10am-5pm, Sat 10am-9pm, Sun 10am-5pm**

### Third Eye Games (2, D4)
A home for hobbyists. You can buy games, from chess games to board games to Dungeons & Dragons and their progeny. You can play games in the back (there's an in-store tournament most Saturdays) or just look on while you check out the animation gear.
✉ **1952 W North Ave, Wicker Park** ☎ **773-342-2957** Ⓣ **Damen** 🚌 **56, 72** ⏰ **noon-9pm**

### Uncle Dan's (4, E3)
An army surplus converted to civilian uses, selling hiking boots, outdoor gear, camping supplies and backpacks for city or country use.
✉ **2440 N Lincoln Ave, Lincoln Park** ☎ **773-477-1918** Ⓣ **Fullerton** 🚌 **8, 22** ⏰ **Mon-Fri 10am-8pm, Sat 10am-7pm, Sun 11am-5pm**

### Urban Gardener (4, F2)
Elegant things for urban and suburban gardens, from simple enameled numbers for gates to splendid teak furniture for decks. A feast for the eyes, whatever the season.
✉ **1006 W Armitage Ave, Old Town** ☎ **773-477-2070** Ⓣ **Armitage** 🚌 **8, 73** ⏰ **Mon-Fri 10am-7pm, Sat 10am-6pm, Sun 11am-5pm**

# places to eat

Chicago has been a meat-and-potatoes town from the beginning. Red meat in particular, Big Portions of corn-fed steaks, barbequed ribs and Central European sausages for the hard-working men and women of the City of the Big Shoulders.

The food scene evolved slowly. Small, good French restaurants and sleek Italian-Italian (as opposed to Italian-American) hotspots appeared in the 1950s and 60s. Then Rich Melman and the Lettuce Entertain You (LEU) people opened RJ Grunt's on Lincoln Park West and the city went wild. LEU understood theater and they understood food. It was a winning combination.

The theater brought people in, the food brought them back. The LEU attitude dominates the food scene today. You'll find touches of theater in restaurant decor. You'll also find branches of successful places up and down town.

LEU aside, the food scene is varied and vibrant. The professional classes fill temples of gastronomy like Charlie Trotter's and the Frontera Grill. They join the immigrant classes at taco palaces, pho stands and noodle shops that have materialized with the new arrivals over the past 20 to 30 years.

A Chicagoan generosity of spirit still prevails, with generous portions, generally served with a smile, and often as not with generous spaces around you.

Richard l'Anson

## How Much?

The symbols used in this chapter indicate the cost of a main course, without drinks, tax or tip:

| | |
|---|---|
| $ | under $10 |
| $$ | $10-19 |
| $$$ | $20-29 |
| $$$$ | over $30 |

Ethnic restaurants, sandwich shops and noodle places are generally under $10. A huge portion of the remainder are $10-19, yet another reflection of the low cost of living in Chicago relative to New York or California.

## Drinks

Most restaurants serve alcohol (the drinking age is 21 and lots of places ask for ID) and most restaurants will serve house wines or a selection of wines by the glass. Wines by the glass are usually better quality. Just watch the prices. You should find a good selection of beers. Chicagoans take beer seriously even though it's not a big brewery town. Look for microbrews, particularly in Lincoln Park hangouts, and imported beers. The tap water is safe and clean, fresh from Lake Michigan.

## Booking Tables

Most, but not all, moderate to high-priced restaurants ($$ and up) take reservations for both lunch and dinner, so call ahead if you can. Many restaurants that take reservations also set seats aside for walk-ins, so do not hesitate to ask. Restaurants that don't take reservations frequently subject customers to long waits (20 minutes or more) so ease into it or find another place.

## Tipping

Tipping is customary in restaurants. Servers expect 15-20% of the check total before tax. Give a little more if the service was exceptional and a little less if it wasn't. Many restaurants add a service charge for parties of six or more. If you're with a group, check the check before you tip. Tipping is optional at coffee bars and places where you place your own order at the counter. Fifty cents or $1 is in order if you ask for something complicated like a double half-caffe latte with nonfat soy milk.

## Opening Hours

Most places to eat are open seven days a week. Sunday night and Monday are the usual closing days for those places that do close. Specific restaurant opening hours are listed in the reviews in this chapter.

## Meal Times

The City that Works starts work early. People have breakfast anywhere between 6-8am, so they can get to work sometime between 7-9am. Most eat breakfast in, particularly in winter. Lunch hour usually starts around noon, the dinner hour at 6pm or 6.30pm. There are Chicagoans who eat later and restaurants stay open to 10-11pm to make sure they get fed, but the rhythm of life here runs an hour earlier than on the East or West Coasts.

### Fair Food

Every summer three to four million Chicagoans fill Grant Park for the 10-day Taste of Chicago fair featuring live music and food, leading to countless cases of blisters and indigestion. If a fair that big does not appeal, there are neighborhood street fairs from June through August at the Taste of Randolph Street (where Randolph meets Halsted St in the West Loop) and the Taste of Lincoln Park (Lincoln Ave near Fullerton) plus fairs with distinctly ethnic flavors. Check the city's website at [e] www.ci.chi.il.us/SpecialEvents for details.

Raymond Hillstrom

# ANDERSONVILLE

### Andie's (3, B7) $
*Middle Eastern*
They didn't name Andersonville after Andie's or vice versa, but there are actually those in the area who think that highly of Andie's Lebanese and Greek cooking from hummus to gyros.
✉ 5253 N Clark St
☎ 773-784-8616
🚇 Berwyn 🚌 22
🕐 Sun-Thurs 10.30am-midnight, Fri & Sat 10.30am-1am ♿ V

### Cousins (3, B7) $
*Turkish*
The Cousins offer Turkish dishes and generic Middle Eastern vegetarian food to the Andersons and other Chicagoans. The pasha room, where you can dine on the floor, is another departure from local norms.
✉ 5203 N Clark St
☎ 773-334-4553
🚇 Berwyn 🚌 22
🕐 Sun-Thurs 10.30am-11pm, Fri & Sat 10.30am-midnight ♿ V

### Tomboy (3, B7) $$
*Modern American*
This simple spot draws sophisticated diners from the North Side and the North Shore, to enjoy food with an edge from shrimps fried in phyllo dough to penne from heaven (try the pasta with fennel sausage and rosemary). BYOB.
✉ 5402 N Clark St
☎ 773-907-0636
🚇 Berwyn 🚌 22
🕐 Sun-Thurs 5-10pm, Fri & Sat 5-11pm V

# GOLD COAST

### Ashkenaz (5, D5) $
*Jewish delicatessen*
This hole-in-the-wall may be the best Jewish delicatessen in the city. If you need a corned beef or matzoh ball fix in a hurry, this is your place. Minimal ambience (most of the business is takeout) but can you really taste ambience, anyway?
✉ 10 E Cedar St
☎ 312-944-5006
🚇 Clark/Division
🚌 22, 36 🕐 Mon-Sat 8am-7pm, Sun 7am-6pm ♿

### Big Bowl (5, D5) $
*Pan-Asian*
Bruce Cost melded Asian and American flavors in Berkeley, California, before he joined forces with LEU to bring Big Bowls (and lots of 'em) to Chicago. Elegant but simple places, with simple starters, lots of noodle dishes and stir-fries you can have cooked to order. Yum.
✉ 6 E Cedar St
☎ 312-640-8888
🚇 Clark/Division
🚌 22, 36 🕐 Sun-Thurs 11.30am-10pm, Fri & Sat 11.30am-midnight ♿ V

### Morton's of Chicago (5, D5) $$$
*steakhouse*
Before there was a Morton's for Hollywood deals and Academy Awards parties, there was this Morton's here, noisy, sometimes smoky, filled with guys eating to their heart's content. In the City of the Big Portions, Morton's has some of the biggest.
✉ 1050 N State St
☎ 312-266-4820
🚇 Clark/Division
🚌 22, 36 🕐 Mon-Sat 5.30-11pm, Sun 5-10pm

# LAKEVIEW WEST/SOUTHPORT

### Bistro Zinc (4, B1) $$
*French*
An unpretentious replication of a French bistro on a quiet stretch of Southport Ave. Light fare in the cafe in the front and hearty food in the restaurant in the back, all of it French in spirit and execution. Sidewalk seating in good weather will make the Francophile all

the more at home.
✉ 3443 N Southport Ave ☎ 773-281-3443
🚇 Southport 🚌 152
🕐 5.30-10pm, (to 11pm Fri & Sat, 9pm Sun); cafe Mon-Thurs 5-10pm, Fri 5-11pm, Sat & Sun 11am-11pm

### Chinalite (4, B1) $
*Chinese*
Not your conventional

Chinese restaurant, Chinalite takes traditional flavors and recipes, and lightens them to reduce the fats and eliminate chemicals. The results are delicious, all the more so when washed down with one of the many microbrews from the bar.
✉ 3457 N Southport Ave ☎ 773-244-0300
🚇 Southport 🚌 152

🕐 Sun-Thurs noon-10pm, Fri & Sat noon-11pm ♿ **V**

### Deleece (4, A1) $
*American*

A good-looking specimen of the stylish cafes that are sprouting in city neighborhoods. Known for Sunday brunch, it's also a smart choice for dinner. Just about anything you could want from pastas to fish to flesh, incorporating flavors and techniques from just about everywhere.

✉ **4004 N Southport Ave** ☎ **773-325-1710** 🚇 **22, 80** 🕐 **Mon-Thurs 5.30-10pm, Fri & Sat 5.30-11pm, Sun 5-9pm; Sun brunch 10.30am-2.30pm** ♿ **V**

### Hi Ricky (4, A1) $
*noodle shop*

Another one of the pan-Asian noodle shops that are appearing all over the better parts of Chicago. Hi Ricky has the same clean space, the same reliable noodles and rice and the same low prices. It also has satays of beef, pork, chicken and shrimp, making this a cross between a noodle

---

---

bar and a yakitori stand.

✉ **3730 N Southport Ave** 🚇 **Addison (Brown, Red), Southport** 🚌 **152** 🕐 **Sun-Thurs 11.30am-10pm, Fri & Sat 11.30am-11pm** ♿ **V**

### Otro Mas (4, B1) $$
*Modern Latin American*

New takes on classic Latin American dishes, sometimes simpler, as with a chili-cured pork tenderloin served up with white beans and rice, sometimes more complicated, as with a tuna taco flavored with papaya and a rosemary-dijon salsa. All in a warm dining room classy enough to have come straight from Crate & Barrel.

✉ **3651 N Southport Ave** ☎ **773-348-3200**

---

🚌 **Southport** 🚌 **152** 🕐 **Sun-Thurs 5-10pm, Fri & Sat 5-11pm; Sun brunch 10am-2pm**

### Tango Sur (4, A1) $$
*Argentine*

Argentines love red meat at least as much as Midwesterners, so this Argentine steakhouse is a natural fit. Start with the empanadas then try the skirt steaks, strip steaks or filets from the grill and savor the flavor of the pampas. BYOB.

✉ **3763 N Southport Ave** ☎ **773-477-5466** 🚇 **Addison (Brown, Red), Southport** 🚌 **152** 🕐 **Mon-Thurs 5-10.30pm, Fri & Sat 5-11.30pm, Sun noon-10.30pm** ♿

---

# CHINATOWN

### Phoenix Restaurant (6, E3) $$
*Chinese*

One of the two places to go for dim sum for breakfast (if you're Chinese) or for lunch (if you're not). Also open in the evenings with a range of South Chinese dishes.

✉ **2137 S Archer Ave** ☎ **312-328-0848** 🚇 **Cermak/Chinatown** 🚌 **24** 🕐 **dim sum 8am-3pm; dinner 3-10pm** ♿ **V**

### Three Happiness (6, E3) $$
*Chinese*

The grand dragon of Chinese restaurants serves dim sum at lunch and popular Cantonese dishes at dinner here and at its branch on Cermak Rd.

✉ **2130 S Wentworth Ave** ☎ **312-791-1228** 🚇 **Cermak/Chinatown** 🚌 **24** 🕐 **Mon-Sat 10am-11pm, Sun 10am-10pm** ♿ **V**

Peter Ptschelinzew

*Dip in for dim sum*

# LAKEVIEW

### Addis Abeba (4, B2) $
*Ethiopian*
Load up your injera, the traditional flat bread of Ethiopia, with spicy dishes of lentils and grains that evoke India and the Middle East, and chow down for a meal as easy on the budget as this quiet space is easy on the nerves.
✉ 3521 N Clark St
☎ 773-929-9383
🚇 Addison 🚌 22
🕐 Mon-Thurs 5-10pm, Fri & Sat 5-11pm, Sun 4-10pm ♿ **V**

### Angelina Ristorante (4, B3) $
*Italian*
There's something about the light inside the two small rooms of this tiny neighborhood place that makes everyone and everything look good. The standard trattoria fare and daily specials are presented with grace and style. Romantic and practical, like Chicago at its best.
✉ 3561 N Broadway
☎ 773-935-5933
🚇 Addison 🚌 22, 152
🕐 5.30-11pm; Sun brunch 10am-3pm

### Ann Sather (4, C2) $
*American*
A plain, homey room with plain, homey food served with grace. This is the original. You'll find the same Swedish and American food in its other locations, particularly the signature cinnamon rolls, but you won't find the same atmosphere.
✉ 929 W Belmont Ave
☎ 773-348-2378
🚇 Belmont 🚌 8, 22, 77 🕐 Sun-Thurs 7am-10pm, Fri & Sat 7am-11pm ♿ **V**

### Brother Jimmy's BBQ (4, D2) $$
*barbeque*
If you want your ribs funky, this is the place. Have a taste-test of baby backs done Northern style, Southern style or smoked, with corn bread and greens and other fixings you won't find in a leather-booth joint. Live blues in the evening for dessert if you have room.
✉ 2909 N Sheffield St
☎ 773-528-0888
🚇 Diversey 🚌 8, 76
🕐 Mon-Fri 5-10pm, Sat 11am-1am, Sun 11am-10pm; bar open later ♿

### Chicago Diner (4, B3) $
*vegetarian*
'Meat Free since 1983' and they mean it. They may be serious but they haven't lost a sense of humor about the struggle to get their carnivore neighbors to abandon hot dogs and ribs for a Seitanic Caesar, a No Meata Fajita or a Nacho Mama.
✉ 3411 N Halsted St
☎ 773-935-6696
🚇 Addison 🚌 8
🕐 11am-10pm, Sat & Sun 10am-10pm ♿ **V**

### Cosi (4, C3) $
*cafe*
Starbucks with food and alcohol. Design your own pita bread sandwiches from a host of tempting ingredients from tandoori chicken to sliced vegies, or have a pita bread pizza baked in the corner while you sink into one of the sofas and watch Lakeview go by outside.
✉ 3201 N Clark St
☎ 773-296-4880
🚇 Belmont 🚌 8, 22, 77
🕐 Sun-Thurs 7am-11pm, Fri-Sun 7am-midnight ♿ **V**

### Erwin (4, D3) $$
*American*
Comfort food with a twist in this noisy bistro. Try the roast chicken with spinach spaetzle or the pan roast halibut with a mushroom cake.
✉ 2925 N Halsted St
☎ 773-528-7200
🚇 Wellington 🚌 8
🕐 Tues-Thurs 5.30-10pm, Fri & Sat 5.30-11pm, Sun 5-9.30pm; Sun brunch 10.30am-2.30pm **V**

### Heaven on Seven on Clark (4, B2) $$
*Cajun/Creole*
The heart of Heaven on Seven is in Louisiana, producing hearty gumbos and jambalayas and savory ribs, while its head keeps drifting overseas, producing Jamaican jerk chicken and coconut-battered shrimp. Something for everyone with a taste for seafood or spices.
✉ 3478 N Clark St
☎ 773-477-7818
🚇 Addison 🚌 22
🕐 Mon-Thurs 5-10.30pm, Fri 5-11pm, Sat 11am-11pm, Sun 11am-10.30pm (open 11am if day game at Wrigley) ♿

### Jack's on Halsted (4, C3) $$
*Modern American*
Mod-Am cooking, borrowing from Italy and Asia to adapt conventional American dishes such as fish, chicken or chops, in a pleasant room that makes the most of its location where Lakeview meets Boystown.
✉ 3201 N Halsted St
☎ 773-244-9191
🚇 Belmont 🚌 8, 22, 36
🕐 Mon-Thurs 5.30-11pm, Fri & Sat 5pm-midnight, Sun 5-10pm **V**

**Joy's Noodles and Rice**
(4, C3) **$**
*Thai*
The sister restaurant of
**Noodles in the Pot** (4, E3;
2453 N Halsted St), Joy's
has the same luscious Thai
noodle and rice dishes in a
luminous space on
Broadway. The lunch specials
are one of the best deals in
the neighborhood.
✉ **3257 N Broadway**
☎ **773-327-8330**
🚇 **Belmont** 🚌 **36, 77**
🕐 **11am-10pm, to**
**11pm Fri & Sat** ♿ **V**

**Matsuya** (4, B3) **$$**
*Japanese*
Half-dozen kinds of
cooked fish are served
most evenings, along with
noodles and tempura and
such, but it's the raw stuff
(sushi, sashimi and hand
rolls) that have locals lin-
ing up night after night.
✉ **3469 N Clark St**
☎ **773-248-2677**
🚇 **Addison** 🚌 **8, 22**
🕐 **Mon-Fri 5-11pm, Sat**
**& Sun noon-11.30pm** **V**

**Melrose Restaurant**
(4, C3) **$**
*coffee shop*
One of a score of North Side
coffee shops that line Lincoln
Ave, Clark St and Broadway,
the Melrose has a theatrical
edge from its location and
its hours . There's the same
choice of basic dishes as the

others, with a better show.
✉ **3233 N Broadway**
☎ **773-327-2060**
🚇 **Belmont** 🚌 **36, 77**
🕐 **24-7** ♿ **V**

**Mohti Matal** (4, C2) **$**
*Indian*
One of the best and most
convenient Indian restaur-
ants on the North Side.
Tandoori dishes and meat-
less curries delight carnivores
and herbivores alike. BYOB.
✉ **1035 W Belmont**
**Ave** ☎ **773-348-4392**
🚇 **Belmont** 🚌 **22, 72**
🕐 **11am-10pm** ♿ **V**

**Nagano** (4, B2) **$**
*Japanese*
Wonderful food, from sushi
and teriyaki dishes to hot
noodle dishes for cold win-
ter nights. Not as crowded
as Matsuya down the block,
and equally appealing.
✉ **3475 N Clark St**
☎ **773-871-2312**
🚇 **Addison** 🚌 **22**
🕐 **lunch Tues-Sun**
**11.30am-2.30pm; dinner**
**Tues-Sat 5-11pm, Sun 5-**
**10pm** ♿ **V**

**The Outpost** (4, B2) **$$**
*Modern American*
A different menu every
month with foods from
around the world, assem-
bled in Mod-Am manner by
Kevin Shikami. The signa-
ture dessert, wontons
stuffed with chocolate and

banana, says it all.
✉ **3438 N Clark St**
☎ **773-244-1166**
🚇 **Addison** 🚌 **22**
🕐 **Mon-Thurs 5.30-**
**10.30pm, Fri & Sat 5.30-**
**11pm, Sun 5-9pm** **V**

**PS Bangkok** (4, C3) **$**
*Thai*
One of the first Thai restaurants to hit Chicago and still
one of the most popular. All
the Thai standards are done
gracefully and priced eco-
nomically. Sunday's grand
buffet may be one of the
best deals in town.
✉ **3345 N Clark St**
☎ **773-871-7777**
🚇 **Addison** 🚌 **22**
🕐 **Tues-Sun 11.30am-**
**10pm (to 11.30pm Fri &**
**Sat)** ♿ **V**

**Salt & Pepper Diner**
(4, B2) **$**
*American*
A faux-diner serving diner
food with beer and wine.
The club sandwiches, burgers and breakfast plates are
straight from the 50s. The
salads are a well-executed
concession to the 21st century. Payment is out of the
50s, too. No credit cards.
✉ **3537 N Clark St**
☎ **773-883-9800**
🚇 **Addison** 🚌 **22**
🕐 **Mon-Thurs 7am-**
**10pm, Fri & Sat 7am-**
**midnight, Sun 7am-4pm**
♿ **V**

## Meatless Meal Tickets

It is possible for vegetarians to survive and even enjoy a
trip to The City of The Big Steak. A handful of places
such as the **Chicago Diner** (p. 74) and the **HeartWise
Express** (p. 78) are either completely or largely vegetarian. Alternatively, try Middle Eastern and Indian
restaurants such as **Cousins** (p. 72), **Tiffin** (p. 86) and
**Mohti Matal** (p. 75), or the Asian or faux-Asian noodle shops that are springing up all around town.

Richard I'Anson

# LINCOLN PARK

### Demon Dogs (4, E2) $
*hot dogs*
One of the better-regarded hot dog stands in the city, in one of the most convenient locations right under the El tracks at Fullerton. Ideal for an early snack on the way to the bars or the clubs along Lincoln.
✉ 944 W Fullerton Ave
☎ 773-281-2001
🚇 Fullerton 🚌 8, 11, 74
🕐 Mon-Fri 6am-10pm, Sat & Sun 10am-8pm ♿

### Café Ba-Ba-Reeba! (4, F3) $$
*Spanish*
The LEU vision of a tapas bar. All the hot and cold dishes you could ask for, including a killer paella, in a chacha series of rooms that make you want to get up on a table with your castanets and dance.
✉ 2024 N Halsted St
☎ 773-935-5000
🚇 Armitage 🚌 8, 73

🕐 Mon-Thurs noon-10pm, Fri & Sat noon-midnight, Sun 10am-5pm ♿ V

### Hanabi (4, E3) $
*Japanese*
A quiet neighborhood restaurant serving sushi, sashimi and the usual hot dishes (tempura, teriyaki and katsu cutlets). Order one of your favorites or try one of theirs, such as the dragon maki (seaweed roll) with eel, avocado and cream cheese.
✉ 806 W Webster Ave
☎ 773-935-3474
🚇 Fullerton 🚌 8, 11, 74 🕐 Mon-Tues & Thurs-Sat 11.30am-2.30pm; Mon, Tues & Thurs 5-10pm, Fri & Sat 5-11pm, Sun 3-9pm ♿

### Mon Ami Gabi (4, E4) $$
*French*
A classic French bistro from the LEU group, serving

bistro standards like four varieties of steak frites, mussels marinere and roast chicken. The setting is French, the food is French, but the service is pure Chicago, so relax.
✉ 2300 N Lincoln Park West ☎ 773-348-8886
🚇 Fullerton 🚌 8, 72
🕐 Mon-Thurs 5.30-10pm, Fri & Sat 5.30-11pm, Sun 5-9pm

### North Pond Café (4, D4) $$$
*American*
This would be one of the most romantic restaurants in Chicago for location alone, in a restored ice skater's shelter in Lincoln Park, looking down North Pond to the city skyline. It's all the more romantic for the glorious Prairie Style interior and the splendid Midwest/American food (Amish chicken, anyone?).
✉ 2610 N Cannon Dr
☎ 773-477-5845
🚇 Fullerton 🚌 22, 36
🕐 Tues-Sat 11am-2pm, Sun 11am-4pm; Tues-Sat 5-9.30pm

### O'Fame (4, E3) $$
*Italian*
The Lincoln Park branch of this set of family-owned restaurants has a dining room as clean, fresh and warm as the family's takes on Italian-American classics from savory minestrones to toothsome pastas to the ubiquitous veal and chicken dishes. Jammed evenings and weekends by the young single set.
✉ 750 W Webster Ave
☎ 773-929-5111
🚇 Fullerton 🚌 8, 11

## Room With a View

The best dining view in town is from the **Signature Room** on the 95th floor of the John Hancock Center (5, E6; ☎ 312-787-9596; open Mon-Thurs 11am-10pm, Fri & Sat 11am-11pm, Sun 10.30am-10pm). **Riva**, at right, on Navy Pier (5, G10; ☎ 312-644-7482; open 11am-midnight) is a close contender, with a view of the city skyline across the water. Also up there are **Everest** (p. 78), **Spiaggia** (p. 81) and the **North Pond Café** (p. 76).

Tom Given

🕐 **Mon-Sat 11am-11pm, Sun 10am-4pm** **V**

### Penny's Noodle Shop (4, D2) $
*noodle shop*
This pan-Asian noodle shop offers tastes of Thai, Chinese and Japanese food in a slick American urban package. Try them here, in Wrigleyville (4, B2; 3400 N Sheffield St) or in Wicker Park (2, D3; 1542 N Damen Ave).
✉ **950 W Diversey Pkwy** ☎ **773-281-8448**
🚇 **Diversey** 🚌 **8, 76**
🕐 **Sun & Tues-Thurs 11am-10pm, Fri & Sat 11am-10.30pm** ⚕ **V**

### Taco & Burrito Palace #2 (4, E3) $
*Mexican*
This six-booth stand produces food good enough for the streets of El Paso. Tacos and burritos as advertised, of grilled steak, pork or chicken with your choice of trimmings, or try the chimichangas (tortillas piled high and covered with cheese). Top it off with the green sauce. Viva!
✉ **2441 N Halsted St**
☎ **772-248-0740**
🚇 **Fullerton** 🚌 **8, 11**
🕐 **Mon, Wed & Thurs 10am-3am, Tues 10am-4am, Fri & Sat 10am-5am** ⚕ **V**

### Toast (4, E3) $
*American*
The hot Lincoln Park breakfast and lunch spot. Relatively conventional breakfast fare competes for diner's dollars with less conventional sandwiches and salads such as a grilled mustard chicken breast sandwich with gruyere and a caesar salad with red potatoes and steak. A very good place for kids.
✉ **746 W Webster Ave**
☎ **773-935-5600**
🚇 **Fullerton** 🚌 **8, 72**
🕐 **Tues-Fri 7am-4pm, Sat & Sun 8am-4pm** ⚕ **V**

# HYDE PARK

### Medici (7, D5) $
*Italian*
This pizza joint near the University of Chicago is a hangout for the neighborhood high school-to-college set. Given the high standards of the area it's no surprise the pizza is as good as the conversation.
✉ **1327 E 57th St**
☎ **773-667-7394**
🚇 **59th St** 🚌 **6**
🕐 **Mon-Thurs 7am-11.30pm, Fri 7am-12.30am, Sat 9am-12.30am, Sun 9am-11.30pm** ⚕ **V**

### Pizza Capri (7, B6) $
*Italian*
Pizza Capri straddles the great culinary divide, offering both Chicago-style pizzas (thin and crispy or stuffed, your choice of ingredients) and gourmet pizzas (Greek toppings, barbeque chicken and vegies among others) here in Hyde Park and at other locations in the city. It also serves pastas and salads.
✉ **1501 E 53rd St**
☎ **773-324-7777**
🚇 **53rd St** 🚌 **6**
🕐 **Mon-Thurs 11am-10.30pm, Fri 11am-11.30pm; brunch Sat & Sun 9am-3pm; dinner Sat 3-11.30pm, Sun 3-10.30pm** ⚕ **V**

# LITTLE ITALY

### Al's Italian Beef (3, E7) $
*Italian*
This is the other famous Italian beef sandwich stand in town. If you can't get out to Little Italy, you could try their version at the River North shop at 169 W Ontario St (5, G4), but then you couldn't polish off your meal with an Italian ice from Mario's across the street.
✉ **1079 W Taylor St**
☎ **312-226-4017**
🚇 **Racine (daytime only)**
🚌 **60** 🕐 **Mon-Sat 9am-1am** ⚕

### Francesca's on Taylor (3, E7) $$
*Italian*
This family of restaurants started in Lakeview with Mia Francesca (4, C3; 3311 N Clark St), then opened in Little Italy. Easy to drive to, it offers a Chicago take on Italian food (big portions, lots of meat). Desserts are delicious and challenging to finish.
✉ **1400 W Taylor St**
☎ **312-829-2828**
🚇 **Racine (daytime only)**
🚌 **60** 🕐 **lunch Mon-Fri 11.30am-2pm; dinner Mon, Tues & Sun 5-9pm, Wed & Thurs 5-10pm, Fri & Sat 5-11pm** ⚕ **V**

# THE LOOP

### Atwood Café
(5, K5) **$$**

*Modern American*

There's a grand view of the center of The Loop out the window here on the ground floor of the Reliance Building, renovated into the Hotel Burnham (p. 102) by San Francisco's Kimpton Group. Modern American food on the tables complements the classic American interior.

✉ **Hotel Burnham, 1 W Washington Blvd**
☎ **312-368-1900**
🚇 **Washington**
🚌 **22, 36** ⏰ **Mon-Fri 7am-10pm, Sat & Sun 8am-10pm** **V**

### The Berghoff
(5, L5) **$$**

*German*

Chicago's oldest restaurant is more than a reminder that the Midwest was once an English-speaking German colony. It's still the place for sensational sauerbraten, potato pancakes and oh-so-German beers, and breads and sausages to eat here or take away.

✉ **17 W Adams St**
☎ **312-427-3170**
🚇 **Jackson** 🚌 **22, 36, 145, 146, 147, 151**
⏰ **Mon-Thurs 11am-9pm, Fri 11am-9.30pm, Sat 11am-10pm** ⚕

### Everest
(5, M4) **$$$**

*French*

Fine French food 40 stories up. A contemporary menu reflecting the Alsatian roots of chef Jean Joho, in a room that would be romantic without a view.

✉ **440 S LaSalle St**
☎ **312-663-9820**
🚇 **LaSalle** 🚌 **156**
⏰ **Tues-Thurs 5.30-9pm, Fri & Sat 5.30-10pm**

### Gold Coast Dogs
(5, J6) **$**

*hot dogs*

One of the great Chicago hot dogs, consistently named one of the best in America. Throw caution to the winds, lather on the garnishes, and add an order of cheese fries lest you get hungry.

✉ **159 N Wabash Ave**
☎ **312-917-1677**
🚇 **Randolph, State, Lake** 🚌 **145, 146, 147, 151** ⏰ **Mon-Fri 10am-8pm, Sat & Sun 10am-5pm** ⚕

### HeartWise Express
(5, K4) **$**

*American*

Some places promote heart-wise dishes, but the HeartWise Express promotes heart-wise thinking, listing the nutritional value of every dish from the noodle and rice bowls to the salads, baked potatoes, wraps and sandwiches. The eye-and-mouth appeal of the dishes on your plate promotes heart-wise eating.

✉ **10 S LaSalle St (enter on Madison St)**
☎ **312-419-1329**
🚇 **Washington (Blue, Brown, Orange)** 🚌 **156**
⏰ **Mon-Fri 6.30am-6pm** ⚕ **V**

*Step back in 'Zeit' at The Berghoff.*

Raymond Hillstrom

## Italian Village Restaurants (5, L5) $$
*Italian*

A fixture in The Loop since 1927, the Italian Village serves up Italian-American dishes that have stood the test of time, like chicken Vesuvio and veal marsala, in a setting that replicates a villa in Italy.

✉ **71 W Monroe St**
☎ **312-332-7005**
⊖ **Monroe** 🚌 **22**
⏰ **Mon-Thurs 11am-1am, Fri & Sat 11am-2am, Sun 11am-midnight** ⚹ **V**

## Mrs Levy's Delicatessen (5, L3) $
*Jewish delicatessen*

Mrs L serves the best corned beef sandwiches in The Loop and triple deckers perfect for her Sears Tower location. Try the Sonnenschein, named for Scott Turow's law firm on the 80th floor, with turkey, bacon, Colby cheese, coleslaw and Russian dressing on challah.

✉ **Sears Tower, 233 S Wacker Dr** ☎ **312-993-0530** ⊖ **Quincy**
🚌 **60, 156** ⏰ **Mon-Fri 6.30am-3pm** ⚹

## Restaurant on the Park (5, L6) $$
*Modern American*

An elegant dining room serving elegant food from a grilled chicken salad with a design degree to grilled veal medallions with black truffles. Worth the detour for a break from a day at the Art Institute, and for the view of Grant Park and the city.

✉ **Art Institute of Chicago, 111 S Michigan Ave** ☎ **312-443-3543**
⊖ **Adams** 🚌 **3, 4, 6, 145, 146, 147, 151** ⏰ **Mon-Sat 11am-2.30pm**

## Rhapsody (5, L6) $$$
*Modern American*

A suitably romantic restaurant built behind the Symphony Center, hence the name. Deft variations on the classics like a roast venison with celery root puree or a sturgeon with roast parsnips. Cafe seating, also available, is particularly handy before a performance or for lunch.

✉ **65 E Adams St**
☎ **312-786-9911**
⊖ **Adams** 🚌 **36, 145, 146, 151** ⏰ **lunch Mon-Fri 11.30am-2pm; dinner Mon-Thurs 5-10pm, Fri & Sat 5-10.30pm, Sun 4.30-9pm**

## Sopraffina Market Café (5, L3) $
*Italian*

A downtown coffee shop with a heavy Italian accent, from the classy design of the space to the menu featuring thin-crust pizzas, pastas, customizable antipasti and gourmet sandwiches on Italian breads with Italian meats and vegies and cheeses. Also at the Illinois Center (5, J8; 200 E Randolph St;).

✉ **222 W Adams St (enter on Franklin St)**
☎ **312-726-4800**
⊖ **Quincy** 🚌 **60, 156**
⏰ **Mon-Fri 6am-4pm** ⚹ **V**

## Trattoria 10 (5, K5) $$
*Italian*

Italian-Italian food in a beautiful space, with updates on classics like seared venison risotto or farfalle pasta with duck confit. Good for lunch, great for dinner before a downtown show.

✉ **10 N Dearborn St**
☎ **312-984-1718**
⊖ **Washington**
🚌 **22, 36, 157**
⏰ **Mon-Fri 11.30am-2pm; Mon-Thurs 5.30-9pm, Fri & Sat 5.30-10pm** **V**

## Zoom Kitchen (5, L5) $
*American*

This is an American cafeteria that could have been designed by Mies van der Rohe's granddaughter (if he had one). American staples like roast turkey, mashed potatoes and meatloaf served with industrial chic. Other locations at 620 W Belmont Ave (4, C3), on the Gold Coast and in Bucktown.

✉ **247 S State St**
☎ **312-337-9666**
⊖ **Jackson, Adams**
🚌 **3, 4, 6, 36, 145, 146, 147, 151**
⏰ **breakfast Mon-Fri 8-10am; lunch & dinner Mon-Fri 11am-6pm, Sat 11am-4pm** ⚹ **V**

*Had an art-fill? Park yourself for eats over Grant Park.*

# NEAR NORTH

## Ben Pao (5, G6) $$
*Chinese*
Rich Melman and LEU go to China. They and their chef-partner Tony Cheung came with boatloads of recipes to delight diners in a grand space that would wow them in the best parts of Hong Kong.
✉ 55 E Illinois St
☎ 312-222-1888
Ⓜ Grand Ⓑ 29, 36
🕐 Mon-Fri 11.30am-4pm; Mon-Thurs 5-10pm, Fri & Sat 5-11pm, Sun 4-9pm ♿

## Blackhawk Lodge (5, F5) $$$
*Modern American*
A real guy's place, featuring game, roast duck, steak and beef in a space designed to actually look like a North Woods resort.
✉ 41 E Superior St
☎ 312-280-4080
Ⓜ Chicago (Red)
Ⓑ 36, 66 🕐 Mon-Fri 11.30am-2pm, Sun 11am-3pm; Mon-Sat 5-10pm, Sun 5-9pm

## Bistro 110 (5, E6) $$
*French*
Classic bistro food from the escargot to the lamb shank to the tarte tartin at the end of the meal. Service gets mixed reviews, as do the waits on weekends.
✉ 110 E Pearson St
☎ 312-266-3110
Ⓜ Chicago (Red)
Ⓑ 66, 145, 146, 147, 151 🕐 Mon-Thurs 11.30am-11pm, Fri & Sat 11.30am-midnight, Sun 11am-10pm ♿ Ⓥ

## Brasserie Jo (5, H5) $$
*French*
One of the hottest spots in town, with splendid renditions of the French brasserie classics from oysters to the duck leg confit, in a room that successfully evokes Paris in the shadow of Mag Mile.
✉ 59 W Hubbard St
☎ 312-595-0808 ○
Ⓜ Grand Ⓑ 36
🕐 lunch Mon-Fri 11.30am-4pm; dinner Mon-Thurs 5-10.30pm, Fri & Sat 5-11.30pm, Sun 4-10pm

## Caliterra (5, F6) $$$
*Modern American*
John Coletta brings an academic edge to the business of eating, asking us to consider warm memories with his winter menu or to ponder the uses of artichokes with his ingredient-of-the-month menus. The result is as satisfying as a docent tour of the Art Institute.
✉ 633 N St Clair St
☎ 312-274-4444
Ⓑ 3, 145, 146, 147, 151 🕐 6am-11pm Ⓥ

## Cheesecake Factory (5, E6) $
*American*
If you've wondered what it looks like inside a cheesecake, run to the concourse level of the John Hancock Center and see. If you only want to taste one of the enormous sandwiches or equally enormous slices of the 30-plus flavors of cheesecake, just walk.
✉ John Hancock Center, 875 N Michigan Ave ☎ 312-337-1101
Ⓜ Chicago (Red)
Ⓑ 145, 146, 147, 151
🕐 Mon-Thurs 11am-11.30pm, Fri & Sat 11am-12.30am, Sun 10am-11pm ♿ Ⓥ

## Frontera Grill/ Topolobampo (5, G4) $$
*Mexican*
Mexican food like you've never had before, taken to new heights by Rick and Deann Groen Bayless. Frontera has tacos, chile rellenos and other updated standards, at modest prices worth the wait for a table. Topolobampo is more expensive, creative and civilized, as it takes reservations.
✉ 445 N Clark St
☎ 312-661-1434
Ⓜ Grand Ⓑ 22
🕐 lunch (Frontera Grill only) Tues-Fri 11am-2.30pm; dinner Tues-Thurs 5-10pm, Fri & Sat 5-11pm Ⓥ

*At the frontier of Mexican cooking in Chicago*

## Johnny Rockets
(5, D5)                    $
*burgers*
Great burgers, shakes and
fries in a replica of a
1950s malt shop com-
plete with Happy Days
music on the jukeboxes
and kids working the
counter wearing clean
white uniforms and little
caps.
✉ 901 N Rush St
☎ 312-337-3900
🚇 Chicago (Red)
🚌 145, 146, 147, 151
🕐 Mon-Thurs 7am-
10pm, Fri & Sat 7am-
midnight, Sun 8am-
10pm ♿

## L'Appetito (5, E6)    $
*Italian*
This sleek little deli may be
the most reasonable place
for a light lunch or an early
dinner on the Mag Mile.
The Italian and American
sandwiches are a good cut
above office building food
and the tostinos (little
grilled sandwiches) will
warm you nicely on a cold
day.
✉ John Hancock Center,
875 N Michigan Ave
☎ 312-337-0691
🚇 Chicago (Red)
🚌 145, 146, 147, 151
🕐 Mon-Fri 7.30am-
7.30pm, Sat & Sun
8.30am-6.30pm ♿ V

## McCormick &
## Schmick's Seafood
## Restaurant
(5, E5)                    $$
*seafood*
McCormick prints the
menu fresh every day so it
can print a list of what's
fresh, from Ecuador tilapia
or Fijian ono to oysters
from Washington State.
Expect lots of good choices
in warm, paneled dining
rooms that give the illusion

## Going to the Dogs
Chicago was famous for hot dogs long before
Americans made the connection between city poli-
tics and sausage-making. The dog was invented here
at the Columbian Exposition in 1893. Today over
2000 hot dog stands dot the city and suburbs.

The locally made Vienna all-beef dog is the stan-
dard, usually served with 'the works' – yellow mus-
tard, relish, pickles, peppers, tomatoes and onions,
even a couple of French fries at old-time stands like
**Fluky's** (which has migrated north with its cus-
tomers to 3333 W Touhy Ave in Lincolnwood; 3, A6;
☎ 847-677-7726). If you order ketchup on your dog
people will know you're from out of town.

If you can't get to **Fluky's** (it has a branch now
in Near North in the Shops at North Bridge; 5, G6)
try the **Gold Coast Dogs** (5, J6) stand in The Loop,
the **Demon Dogs** (4, E2) stand under the Fullerton
El station, or go to the source – there's a stand at
the **Vienna factory** at 2501 N Damen Ave (3, C7;
☎ 773-278-7800).

they've been there forever.
✉ 41 E Chestnut St
☎ 312-397-9500
🚇 Chicago (Red)
🚌 36 🕐 Sun-Thurs
11.30am-midnight, Fri
& Sat 11.30am-2am

## Pizzeria Uno (5, G5)  $
*Italian*
This is where the infamous
Chicago Deep Dish Pizza
was invented, by Ike Sewell
in 1943. You can find fran-
chises and imitations all
across North America these
days, but this is where it all
began (for better or worse).
✉ 29 E Ohio St
☎ 312-321-1000
🚇 Grand 🚌 36
🕐 Mon-Fri 11.30am-
1am, Sat 11.30am-2am,
Sun 11.30am-11.30pm
♿ V

## Spiaggia (5, D6)  $$$$
*Italian*
There isn't a bad seat in
the house here, overlooking
Michigan Ave and the Oak

St Beach, and there's hardly
a bad choice on the menu,
where Paul Bertolotta pres-
ents deceptively simple
Italian dishes that show
that in food, as in architec-
ture, less can be more.
✉ 980 N Michigan Ave
☎ 312-28-02750
🚇 Chicago (Red)
🚌 145, 146, 147, 151
🕐 lunch Mon-Sat
11.30am-2pm; dinner
Mon-Thurs 5.30-
9.30pm, Fri & Sat 5.30-
10.30pm, Sun 5.30-9pm

## West Egg Café (5, G7)  $
*coffee shop*
A coffee shop serving
breakfast and lunches in a
space and a manner almost
untouched since the 1940s.
Don't expect anything
fancy, least of all a fancy
bill when you're done.
✉ 620 N Fairbanks Ct
☎ 312-280-6366
🚌 66, 157 🕐 Mon-Fri
6.30am-3pm, Sat & Sun
7am-4pm ♿

# OLD TOWN

## Charlie Trotter's
(4, F3) $$$
*Modern American*
Charlie Trotter is the star of the Chicago food scene, winner of the 1999 James Beard award as best chef in America. Book early, dress up and come on in for one of his extraordinary degustation menus.
✉ 816 W Armitage Ave
☎ 773-248-6228
Ⓜ Armitage 🚍 8, 73
🕐 Tues-Sat 5.30-11pm

## The Fireplace Inn
(5, B4) $$
*barbeque*
One of the places on everyone's short list of the best rib joints in town, serving baby backs and beef ribs marinated and barbequed and served dry with sauce on the side if you need any. The scene, a 60s-style room with red leather booths and Sinatra on the sound system, is as satisfying as the food.
✉ 1448 N Wells St
☎ 312-664-5264
Ⓜ Clark/Division, Sedgwick 🚍 156
🕐 Mon-Thurs 4-10pm, Fri & Sat 4-11pm, Sun 1-10pm ♿

## Geja's Café (4, F4) $$
*fondue*
Not one for the lactose-intolerant, Geja's is filled with couples gazing into each other's eyes over their fondue pots as the guitar strums in the background, all very romantic regardless of what one may think about cheese. No children under 10 (there's all that hot oil on the tables).
✉ 340 W Armitage Ave
☎ 773-281-9101

Ⓜ Sedgwick
🚍 22, 36, 151
🕐 Mon-Thurs 5-10.30pm, Fri 5pm-midnight, Sat 5pm-12.30am, Sun 4.30-10pm

## King Crab Tavern & Seafood Grill
(4, F3) $$
*seafood*
This is a seafood house crossed with a Cajun roadhouse and the combination isn't half bad. The oysters are fresh and delicious, the best reason to go.
✉ 1816 N Halsted St
☎ 312-280-8990
Ⓜ North/Clybourn, Armitage 🚍 8
🕐 Mon-Thurs & Sun 11.30am-11pm, Fri & Sat 11.30am-midnight ♿

## Nookies (4, F4) $
*coffee shop*
'Fresh and friendly' Nookies serves breakfast all day long. You can also get a great open-faced hot beef or turkey sandwich with mashed potatoes and gravy, a salad or even a slice of meatloaf if your body clock says it's too late (or too early) for eggs. Cash only.
✉ 1746 N Wells St
☎ 312-337-2454
Ⓜ Sedgwick 🚍 72, 156
🕐 Mon-Sat 6.30am-10pm, Sun 6.30am-9pm ♿ Ⓥ

## ¡Salpicon! (5, C4) $$
*Mexican*
Patricia Satkoff grew up in Mexico City, and she can go mano-a-mano with anyone to produce some of the most inventive Mexican food on either side of the border. If you have a

problem with spices, tell your server.
✉ 1252 N Wells St
☎ 312-988-7811
Ⓜ Clark/Division, Sedgwick 🚍 156
🕐 Sun-Thurs 5-10pm, Fri & Sat 5-11pm; Sun brunch 11am-2.30pm ♿ Ⓥ

## Stanley's Kitchen & Tap (4, F4) $
*American*
The name says it all. The comfort of a bar and comfort food from the kitchen, from chicken fried steak and chicken fried chicken to pot roast and meatloaf and burgers. Dorm food (only better) for a largely 20-something post-collegiate crowd.
✉ 1970 N Lincoln Ave
☎ 312-642-0007
Ⓜ Sedgwick
🚍 11, 22, 36, 73
🕐 Mon & Tues 5-11pm, Wed-Sun 11am-11pm; bar open to 2am daily

## Vinci (4, F3) $$
*Italian*
Come before a show at the Steppenwolf or the Royal George down the block, or come after the pre-curtain rush for a country-style meal. Try the ribolitta, an antipasti or a half-order of pasta as a starter, to leave room for a main and dessert.
✉ 1732 N Halsted St
☎ 312-266-1199
Ⓜ North/Clybourn
🚍 8 🕐 Tues-Thurs 5.30-10pm, Fri & Sat 5.30-11pm, Sun 3.30-9.30pm; Sun lunch 10.30am-2.30pm Ⓥ

# RIVER NORTH

### Carson's (5, G4)  $$
*barbeque*
One of the most famous ribs joints in town. They generally come wet here, slathered with a tangy sweet sauce. Quiet, almost formal decor unchanged since the days the first Mayor Daley ate here with his pals.
✉ 612 N Wells St
☎ 312-280-9200
Ⓣ Chicago (Brown)
🚌 156 ⏰ Mon-Thurs 11am-11pm, Fri 11am-12.30pm, Sat noon-12.30pm, Sun noon-11pm ♿

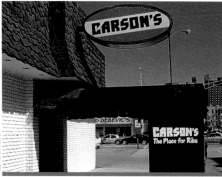

If it's ribs you want, head to Carson's.

### Coco Pazzo (5, H4)  $$$
*Mediterranean*
This is northern Italian cooking the way Chicagoans like to eat, with hearty main dishes of venison, game birds and beef with savory pastas to begin. Big with the business set. A less formal variant on the theme is available at Coco Pazzo Café (5, G6; 636 N St Clair St)
✉ 300 W Hubbard St
☎ 312-836-0900
Ⓣ Merchandise Mart
🚌 156 ⏰ Mon-Fri 11.30am-2.30pm; Mon-Thurs 5.30-10.30pm, Fri & Sat 5.30-11pm, Sun 5-10pm Ⓥ

### Gene & Georgetti (5, G3)  $$$
*steakhouse*
They say it's the first great steakhouse in town, and heaven knows there are people who've been coming here since it opened in the 1940s. Regulars prefer the smoking section downstairs, so you may have to settle for nonsmoking upstairs. Wherever you sit, be sure to order yours medium-rare.
✉ 500 N Franklin St
☎ 312-527-3718
Ⓣ Merchandise Mart
🚌 156 ⏰ Mon-Sat 11am-midnight

### Mr Beef (5, G3)  $
*Italian*
Handcarved Italian beef sandwiches, slapped on a roll and smothered with roasted red peppers, are a local specialty and Mr Beef is specially known for them. Your eyes and nose will tell you you're in the right place even if the celebrity photos plastered along the walls don't. Cash only.
✉ 666 N Orleans St
☎ 312-337-8500
Ⓣ Chicago (Brown)
🚌 156 ⏰ Mon-Fri 7am-4.45pm, Sat 10am-2pm ♿

### Nacional 27 (5, F3)  $$
*Cuban*
LEU go to Cuba this time, and come back (as always) with a winning formula. Try the traditional pulled pork sandwich or an adaptation like grilled salmon with mango barbeque sauce. Stay for the music and dancing late Friday and Saturday and you won't be disappointed.
✉ 325 W Huron St
☎ 312-664-2727
Ⓣ Chicago (Brown)
🚌 66 ⏰ Mon-Thurs 5.30-10pm, Fri & Sat 5-11pm, Sun 5-9.30pm; bar open till later

## Dealing & Dining
If you have big business downtown, think about **Everest** (p. 78) or **Prairie** in the Hyatt on Printer's Row (5, M5; 500 S Dearborn; ☎ 312-663-1143; open for breakfast, lunch & dinner Mon-Sat 5-10pm, Sun 5-9pm). If the guys (and we do mean guys) want steaks and lobsters or such, it's time for **Gene & Georgetti** (p. 83) or **Morton's** (p. 72).

# WEST LOOP

**Lou Mitchell's**
(5, M2)                                    $
*coffee shop*
A Chicago institution that has earned its reputation. A regular coffee shop down the street from Union Station, it bakes its own bread and pastries and bakes them well, even handing them out to customers waiting in line for breakfast or lunch.

✉ 565 W Jackson Blvd
☎ 312-939-9111
🅱 Clinton (Blue)
🚌 156, 157 ⏱ Mon-Sat 5.30am-3pm, Sun 7am-3pm ⚇ Ⅴ

**Robinson's No 1 Ribs**
(5, L2)                                   $$
*barbeque*
Charley Robinson won first prize in Mike Royko's first barbeque contest and used his 15 minutes of fame to open a little rib joint. It's a big rib joint now and there are branches downtown (5, M5; 77 W Jackson Blvd) and

### Kid's Meals
The early meal times and easy-going attitudes make Chicago a good place to feed kids. You'll find food courts all around, from the **Museum of Science & Industry** (p. 24) and the **Navy Pier** (p. 25) to the **Thompson Center** (p. 35) in The Loop. Before you succumb to the temptation of **Rock & Roll McDonald's** (p. 47), consider the genteel pleasures of a meal in the **Walnut Room** at Marshall Field's (p. 59), where there are coloring books to keep the kids occupied.

uptown (4, F3; 655 W Armitage Ave).
✉ 255 S Canal St
☎ 312-258-8477
🅱 Clinton (Blue)
🚌 156, 157
⏱ 10.30am-9pm ⚇

**Wishbone** (3, E7)      $
*Cajun/soul food*
This large industrial space near Oprah Winfrey's Harpo Studios dishes up Southern comforts such as corn bread muffins and chicken fried steak three

times a day. An optional cafeteria line at lunch helps keep the crowds in control. Also in Lakeview at 3300 N Lincoln Ave (4, C1).
✉ 1001 W Washington Blvd ☎ 312-850-2663
🚌 20 ⏱ breakfast Mon-Fri 7-11am; lunch Mon-Fri 11am-3pm; dinner Tues-Thurs 5-10pm, Fri & Sat 5-11pm, Sun 5-9pm; brunch Sat & Sun 8.30am-2.30pm ⚇ Ⅴ

*Standing room only at Lou Mitchell's*

# WICKER PARK/BUCKTOWN

### Bongo Room (2, D4) $
*American*
Some days it seems like half of Wicker Park is also waiting for a table in this bright, sunny space. The food is good and the scene is even better. It's mainly a breakfast and brunch place, but you can get salads and sandwiches at lunchtime during the week.
✉ 1470 N Milwaukee Ave ☎ 773-489-0690 ⊖ Damen 🚌 56, 66 ⏰ Mon-Fri 8am-2.30pm, Sat & Sun 9.30am-2.30pm ♿ V

### Café Absinthe (2, D4)    $$$
*Modern American*
One of fanciest spots in Wicker Park, serving the standards (main courses fish, chicken, steak among others) with a world-music sensibility (try grated coconut on your chicken, you'll like it). The soul and funk soundtrack in the background adds the final touch of cross-cultural innovation.
✉ 1954 W North Ave (entrance in the alley off Damen Ave) ☎ 773-278-4488 ⊖ Damen 🚌 50, 56, 72 ⏰ 5.30-10pm

### Café Lucky (2, C4)    $
*Italian*
Italian-American, including Sicilian-American, food dished out in a dining room that recalls a swank spot in the 1940s. Look for standards like martinis at the bar in the front (the cheese-stuffed olives are a signature item), veal parmesan on the menu and Frank on the jukebox.
✉ 1824 W Wabanasia Ave ☎ 773-227-2300 ⊖ Damen 🚌 72 ⏰ Mon-Thurs 11.30am-11pm, Fri 11.30am-midnight, Sat 5pm-midnight, Sun 4-10pm; lounge open till later ♿ V

### Commune Café (2, D3)    $
*American*
American coffee shop food suitably adapted for stylish surroundings in the heart of Wicker Park hipness, such as macaroni and cheese with oven dried tomatoes, green onions and parmesan or Cuban-style fried chicken. Great range of choices for vegetarians to boot.
✉ 1616 N Damen Ave ☎ 773-772-7100 ⊖ Damen 🚌 50, 56, 72 ⏰ Mon-Fri 9am-10pm, Sat & Sun 9am-11pm V

### Ezuli (2, D4)    $
*Caribbean*
French-Caribbean fare like bass with red-bean cakes and Caribbean favorites like Jamaican jerked catfish in a fresh space on the Milwaukee Ave strip that stays open late. DJ tunes from 10pm nightly.
✉ 1415 N Milwaukee Ave ☎ 773-227-8200 ⊖ Damen 🚌 50, 56, 72 ⏰ 6pm-2am (kitchen open to 1.30am) V

### Local Grind (2, D4)    $
*coffee shop*
Defiantly local in the face of the nearby Starbucks, Local Grind does all the coffee drinks you'd expect from the name, as well as breakfast all day and salads and sandwiches (mainly vegetarian) from midday on. Come hang and watch the Wicker Park world go by.
✉ 1585 N Milwaukee Ave ☎ 773-489-3490 ⊖ Damen 🚌 50, 56, 72 ⏰ Mon-Thurs 6am-midnight, Fri 6am-3am, Sat 7am-3am, Sun 7am-midnight ♿ V

### Dinner for One
There's not a huge number of places with big bars or counters for solo diners, and the big communal tables that are the rage in New York have not caught on here. Some places with decent counters for a traveler eating alone include **Bongo Room** (p. 85) and **Café Lucky** (p. 85) in Bucktown/Wicker Park, and the **Melrose** (p. 75) and **Bistro Zinc** (p. 72) in Lakeview.

### MOD (2, D3)    $$$
*Modern American*
This place is so modern and sleek, an electric orange and blue homage to Rae & Charles Eames, that it's hard to believe you're in Wicker Park. The food is as refined as the space with choices like duck roast with pancetta and espresso-enhanced short ribs.
✉ 1520 N Damen Ave ☎ 773-252-1500 ⊖ Damen 🚌 50, 56, 72 ⏰ Sun-Thurs 5-11pm, Fri & Sat 5pm-midnight V

### Soju (2, D5) $$

*Korean*

Soju demonstrates that 'elegant Korean food' is no oxymoron. Ask them to surprise you if you're adventuresome, order the Soju chicken (deep-fried, with a sauce of hot bean paste and rice wine) if you're not.

✉ 1745 W North Ave
☎ 773-782-9000
🚇 Damen 🚌 56, 72
🕐 Wed & Thurs 6-11pm, Fri & Sat 6pm-midnight, Sun 5-10pm V

### Souk (2, D4) $$

*Middle Eastern*

The chic side of the Middle East in the hip zone of the Middle West. One of the most elegant small rooms in the city, purple walls with leather-topped tables under Futurama lights. Perhaps the best Middle Eastern food in the city, delivered with the same style and grace.

✉ 1552 N Milwaukee Ave ☎ 773-227-9110
🚇 Damen 🚌 50, 56, 72
🕐 5.30pm-2am V

### Soul Kitchen (2, D4) $$

*Cajun*

The oyster bar and the 'new Southern' cooking keep this place constantly packed with locals and people from outside the neighborhood lining up for pecan-coated catfish, vegetable jambalaya and other tangy treats.

✉ 1576 N Milwaukee Ave ☎ 773-342-9742
🚇 Damen 🚌 50, 56, 72
🕐 Sun-Thurs 5-10.30pm, Fri & Sat 5-11.30pm; Sun brunch 10am-4pm V

## UPTOWN/FAR NORTH SIDE

### Arun's (3, B6) $$$$

*Thai*

You'll need wheels and a fat wallet to visit the best Thai restaurant, some say the best Asian, in town. When you get there relax and let the 12-course menu of the day unfold.

✉ 4156 N Kedzie St
☎ 773-539-1909
🚉 N Lake Shore Dr to Irving Park Rd, west on Irving Park Rd to Kedzie, north on Kedzie
🕐 Tues-Sat 5-10pm, Sun 5-9pm ♿

### Pasteur (3, B7) $$

*Vietnamese*

It may be cold outside, but step into Pasteur and the warmth of an old Vietnam that was probably never really this charming. Then the food arrives, from delicate starters to the mains (mainly seafood or poultry, some with a French touch like the Saigonese duck).

✉ 5525 N Broadway
☎ 773-878-1061
🚇 Bryn Mawr
🚌 36 🕐 Mon & Tues 5-10pm, Wed, Thurs-Sun noon-10pm ♿ V

### Pho 777 The House of Noodle (3, B7) $

*Vietnamese*

Don't be put off by the green neon lighting when you step inside the door. Look at the steaming bowls of pho (beef noodle soup) on all the tables and all the happy faces. Expect a short line even when the other pho shops on the block are empty.

✉ 1065 W Argyle St
☎ 773-561-9909
🚇 Argyle 🚌 36
🕐 Mon, Tues & Thurs 9am-8.30pm, Fri 9am-10pm, Sat 8.30am-10pm, Sun 8.30am-9.30pm ♿ V

### Tiffin (3, A7) $

*Indian*

Generally considered the best Indian restaurant in town, Tiffin's upmarket decor belies its downmarket prices (even before one considers the 'deal of the day' and the buffet at lunchtime). Worth the trip for anyone with a craving for biryani or mulligatawny.

✉ 2536 W Devon Ave
☎ 773-338-2143
🚌 36 🕐 lunch 11.30am-3.30pm; dinner Sun-Thurs 5.30-10pm, Fri & Sat 5.30-10.30pm ♿ V

### A Fine Romance

The Windy City has lots of warm spaces for quiet moments. **Geja's Café** (p. 82) tops all the lists, whether for the setting, the guitars or the bubbling fondue pots, who's to say. Everyone loves the dim and cozy rooms of **Angelina Ristorante** (p. 74) because they're dim and cozy and everyone loves **Spiaggia** (p. 81) because everyone looks like a Milan model in this space. If you have a tough nut to crack or a serious question to pop, locals swear that the candlelit glow of the **North Pond Café** (p. 76) will melt any heart.

# entertainment

Fast jazz bands hailed Chicago as 'That Toddlin' Town' in the early 20th century, and at the beginning of the 21st century you can still see a man dance with his wife here, in the town that Billy Sunday couldn't shut down.

Music is the still the mainstay of nightlife. Jazz and the blues came of age here in the Teens and the Twenties, as African-Americans landed in South Side clubs from Memphis and New Orleans and places in between. Today, jazz and the blues are on the playbill from one side of town to the other. Classical music traditions arrived with German immigrants in the 1800s. By the end of the century, the WASP social elite formed and funded a symphony that remains a world class institution today. Rock arrived here as elsewhere in the 1950s, and today you can hear big names and new names in rock, alternative and world music in spaces from the Hothouse downtown to the Aragon Ballroom uptown.

The boom in Chicago theater has been the big story of the past twenty years. Any given week

## Bookings

Most theaters take bookings directly over the phone. The League of Chicago Theaters operates seven **Hot Tix** booths selling half-price that-day tickets to dozens of shows and Ticketmaster tickets to concerts, shows and sporting events. You can check what's available at **e** www .hottix.org or at the in-town booths at 78 W Randolph St, The Loop (5, K5), on the Mag Mile at 163 E Pearson St (5, E6), or inside the Tower Records Stores at 214 S Wabash Ave (5, L6) and 2301 N Clark St (4, E4). All locations take credit cards for all tickets.

Richard Cummins

## Listings

Any week of the year Chicago has hundreds of shows and performances competing for your time and attention. The weekly edition of **The Reader** has the most comprehensive and comprehensible list of theaters, nightclubs and bars. The **Chicago Tribune** Friday entertainment section has the next-best lists. The **Chicago Free Press** and the **Windy City Times** carry current lists of gay and lesbian events, and the Tribune Co Web site, **Metromix**, **e** www.metromix.com, is a great complement to the schedules in the papers.

you'll find a hundred or more listings in the theater sections of the local papers, from big shows headed to or from Broadway to small shows from one of the great non-profit companies like Steppenwolf or the Goodman.

If the music or the shows get your motor running, you can still dance with your wife, or your partner or even a stranger at one of the dance clubs that Chicago has to offer. Billy Sunday (an evangelist preacher who hated liquor and dance halls, in case you're wondering) is long gone, but Chicago keeps toddlin' on.

## SPECIAL EVENTS

**January** *Chinese New Year* – date varies from late Jan to early Feb; parades and firecrackers in Chinatown

**February** *Black History Month* – special displays and exhibits all across town

**March** *St Patrick's Day Parade* – Mar 17; Irish-Americans march down Dearborn St from the banks of the Chicago River, dyed green for the day

**April** *Spring Flower Show* – blooms fill the Garfield Park and Lincoln Park Conservatories all month

**May** *Neighborhood Festivals* – these begin in earnest all around town; check the Mayor's Office of Special Events (☎ 312-744-3315) for details.

**June** *Chicago Gospel Festival, Chicago Blues Festival, Chicago Country Music Festival* – fill Grant Park one weekend each

*Taste of Chicago* (pictured below) – last week June-1st week Jul; three million people eating street food and listening to live music in Grant Park

*Andersonville Midsommerfest* – mid-month; street fair along Clark above Foster

*Gay & Lesbian Pride Parade* – last Sun; through Lakeview

**July** *Independence Day* – Jul 3; concert in Grant Park featuring the '1812 Overture' and fireworks over the water on the eve of the national holiday

*World's Largest Block Party* – 3rd weekend; a singles party sponsored by Old St Patrick's Church in the West Loop

*Venetian Night* – late in the month; yacht owners at Monroe St Harbor decorate their craft, parade them along the lakefront and end the evening with fireworks

**August** *Chicago Air and Water Show* – 3rd weekend; military jets, aerobatic planes and speedboats at Diversey Harbor south to the Oak St Beach

*North Halsted Days street festival* – Boystown celebration

**September** *Viva! Chicago* – usually mid-month; Latin festival in Grant Park

*German American Oktoberfest* – 3rd weekend; in Lincoln Square

**October** *Chicago International Film Festival* – one week during the month

**November** *Magnificent Mile Lights Festival* – mid-month; lighting of hundreds of thousands of lights on the trees for the holiday season

*Official Tree Lighting* – 4th Thurs; Thanksgiving Day at Daley Plaza

# BARS & PUBS

### Artful Dodger (2, C5)
A cozy neighborhood bar on a quiet Wicker Park/Bucktown side street, filled with locals on weeknights and crowds of outsiders on weekends, drawn by the selection of beers, the rest of the crowd and the little dance floor in the back of the back.

✉ 1734 W Wabanasia Ave, Wicker Park
☎ 312-227-6859
🚇 Damen 🚌 72
🕐 Sun-Fri 5pm-2am, Sat 8pm-3am

*Don't let the Artful Dodger lead you astray.*

### Bar 3 (4, E3)
This is a Lincoln Park bar that's not a sports bar or a frat boy hangout. The Crate & Barrel interior and the music (which leans toward funk, soul and R & B) set the place apart from the numerous other watering holes in the neighborhood.

✉ 2138 N Halsted St, Lincoln Park ☎ 773-348-3665 🚇 Armitage 🚌 8 🕐 Sun-Fri 5pm-2am, Sat 5pm-3am

### Border Line Tap (2, D4)
A comfortable local tavern that so far still has room for everyone in Wicker Park, despite the wave of money hitting the neighborhood (exemplified by Café Absinthe next door, owned by the same people).

✉ 1958 W North Ave, Wicker Park ☎ 773-278-5138 🚇 Damen 🚌 50, 56, 72 🕐 Sun-Fri 1pm-4am, Sat 1pm-5am

### Goose Island Brew Pub (4, F2)
The biggest and best-known brew pub in Chicago produces over 40 kinds of beer. There's food to eat if you get hungry, 25 pool tables, and brewery tours (Wed 6pm, Sun 3pm) if you get bored.

✉ 1800 N Clybourn Ave, Old Town
☎ 312-226-1119
🚇 North/Clybourn
🕐 Mon-Thurs 11am-12.30am, Fri & Sat 11am-1.30am, Sun 10am-12.30am

### John Barleycorn Memorial Pub (4, E3)
A Chicago institution since it was opened by an Irish cop in the 1890s, the John Barleycorn still draws everyone in the area from DePaul students to Lincoln Park West cliff dwellers for the beers, the burgers and the atmosphere. Very crowded on weekends.

✉ 658 W Belden Ave, Lincoln Park ☎ 773-348-8899 🚇 Fullerton 🚌 8, 11, 72 🕐 Mon-Fri 4pm-2am, Sat 9am-3am, Sun 9am-2am

### Marquee Lounge
(4, F3) An easy-going neighborhood place where Old Town meets Lincoln Park, attracting North Side 20-somethings and a smattering of other locals. Sample the beers and microbrews on tap, hang out, and maybe play a little pool on the table in the back.

✉ 1967 N Halsted St, Old Town ☎ 773-988-7427 🚇 Armitage 🚌 8 🕐 Mon-Fri 4pm-2am, Sat & Sun 11.30am-2am

### Southport Lanes & Billiards (4, C1)
There's retro and then there's the 1920s preserved to today. Walk on in, get a beer and wander into the side room where you'll find four old-fashioned bowling lanes, pins still set by hand ($14/game and $1.50 for shoes), and six regulation pool tables ($9/hr, $12/hr after 8pm weekends).

✉ 3325 N Southport Ave, Lakeview West/Southport ☎ 773-472-6600 🚇 Southport 🚌 77 🕐 Mon-Fri 4pm-2am, Sat noon-3am, Sun noon-2am

### Sterch's (4, E3)
In the middle of the Mardi Gras madness of the Lincoln Ave bar belt, a sign in the window: 'No Corona. No Foolish Drinks. Limited Dancing. Open to 2am except for…' If your name's not on the list, welcome to Sterch's.

✉ 2238 N Lincoln Ave,

Lincoln Park ☎ 773-281-2653 ⊝ Fullerton 🚌 8, 11 ⏲ 3.30pm-2am

**Webster Wine Bar**
(4, 1E) The best wine bar in town; a warm, romantic room filled with sofas and comfy chairs. Over 40 wines by the glass to sample, with fancy bar food like goat cheese crostini for ballast if you're planning on making a night of it.
✉ 1480 W Webster Ave, Lincoln Park ☎ 773-868-0608 🚌 74 ⏲ Mon-Fri 5pm-2am, Sat 4pm-3am, Sun 4pm-2am

## Rules of the Road

The drinking age in Illinois is 21 and people actually care. You'll need a photo ID to get into most clubs even if you are manifestly over the magic age. Most clubs stop serving at 2am (3am Sat), except for clubs with a '4am license,' which stay open to 4am (5am Sat).

The police are generally easy-going, but don't try their patience with stupid behavior. Drinking under the influence of alcohol or marijuana will win you a trip through the local legal system.

*No ID, no green light in this town (see p. 96-7 for venues)*

# DANCE CLUBS

**Biology Bar** (4, G3)
One of the new clubs that has colonized the strip below the North/Clybourn Red Line station, bringing a certain Lettuce Entertain You (LEU) sensibility to the dance club scene. This one plays a hot Latin soundtrack in a cool futuristic space and packs the 20-somethings in with the combo.
✉ 1520 Fremont St, Old Town ☎ 312-397-0580 ⊝ North/Clybourn 🚌 72 ⏲ Wed-Fri 9pm-4am, Sat 9pm-5am

**Circus** (4, G2)
If the Disney people did serious dance clubs, they'd probably look something like this – a massive set of spaces filled with cartoonish images from the circus world and live circus performers working the dance floor.
✉ 901 W Weed St, Old Town ☎ 312-266-1200 🅴 www.circuschicago.com ⊝ North/Clybourn 🚌 72 ⏲ Thurs & Fri 8pm-4am, Sat 8pm-5am

**Crobar** (4, G2)
The best club in the city, whether mixed (Wed-Sat) or gay (Sun). It's partly the space, designed for drama with levels of dance floors and lounges. It's partly the music, with the best DJs from everywhere. The result is pure energy.
✉ 1543 N Kingsbury St, Old Town ☎ 312-413-7000 ⊝ North/Clybourn 🚌 72 ⏲ Wed-Fri & Sun 10pm-4am, Sat 10pm-5am

**Déjà Vu** (4, D2)
Is this a singles bar with a small dance floor or a small dance club with a large bar filled with singles? Decide for yourself. Enjoy the great mix of music and the great mix of people (skewed heavily, as elsewhere in Lincoln Park, to the 20-somethings).
✉ 2624 N Lincoln Ave, Lincoln Park ☎ 773-871-0205 ⊝ Diversey 🚌 11 ⏲ Sun-Fri 6.30pm-4am, Sat 6.30pm-5am

**Kustom** (4, F2)
The space that was occupied by Liquid has been remodeled and rechristened Kustom. Where salsa and swing swung, now the dolled-up get down to the house sounds of the moment. Your best bet for glitz and glamour (with a little attitude on the side) for a night on the town.
✉ 1997 N Clybourn Ave, Old Town ☎ 773-528-3400 ⊝ North/Clybourn ⏲ Thurs & Fri 9pm-2am, Sat 9pm-3am

**Le Passage** (5, D5)
Down the alley behind Le Colonial, a bar and dance club for fashion plates, models and men who date models. The surroundings are as elegant and as done up as the customers. The Gold Coast location and prices skew the demographics higher than the typical dance club.
✉ One Oak Pl, Gold Coast ☎ 312-255-0022

Ⓞ Clark/Division
🚌 36 🕐 Mon-Wed
6pm-2am, Thurs & Fri
6pm-4am, Sat 6pm-5am

**Red Dog** (2, D4)
First runner-up to Crobar in
the best club award, for the
quality of the crowd as much
as anything else, and they
must be doing something
right to attract Goths and
celebrities to the same place
at the same time. Gay on
Monday nights; otherwise, a
little bit of everything.
✉ **1958 W North Ave,
Wicker Park**
☎ **773-278-1009**
Ⓞ **Damen** 🚌 **50, 56, 72**
🕐 **Mon-Fri 10pm-4am,
Sat 10pm-5am**

**rednofive** (3, E7)
'red number five' is a new
kid on the block, making a
mark with its location in
the wilds of West Loop,
with the music (salsa Wed,
house the rest of the time)
and the late closing hours,
which makes it popular for
workers in the bar business.
✉ **440 N Halsted St,
West Loop** ☎ **312-733-
6699** Ⓞ **Clinton (Green)**
🚌 **56** 🕐 **Tues-Sun
10pm-4am (until 5am Sat)**

**Smart Bar** (4, A2)
The extraordinary range of
extraordinarily good music
here, from hip hop to tech-
no to retro to ska, is understandable given its location

in the basement of the
Metro, which hosts some
of the town's best live acts.
✉ **3730 N Clark St,
Wrigleyville** ☎ **773-
549-4140** Ⓞ **Addison**
🚌 **22, 152** 🕐 **9pm-4am**

**Spy Bar** (5, G3)
This is one of the glam gardens that have grown up
in and around River North.
There's a huge bar, a
lounge and a dance floor
for moving to house and
hip hop. High marks for
high style and low attitude.
✉ **646 N Franklin St,
River North** ☎ **312-587-
8779** Ⓞ **Chicago
(Brown)** 🚌 **66** 🕐 **Tues,
Thurs-Sat 10.30pm-5am**

# CINEMAS

**Esquire Theater** (5, D6)
Inside the skin of this
1920s neighborhood movie
theater lurks the heart and
screening rooms of a mod-
ern six-screen Cineplex.
What has been lost in the
way of charm has been
retained in the way of
convenience, given the
location right at the top of
the Magnificent Mile.
✉ **58 E Oak St, Gold
Coast** ☎ **312-280-0101**
🅔 **www.loewscineplex
.com** Ⓞ **Clark/Division**
🚌 **145, 146, 147, 151** ⚤

**Facets Multimedia**
(4, E1) Not for the middle-
brow, Facets shows indie
foreign and domestic films
that don't always get commercial distribution, in its
125-seat movie theater. It
also shows films shot in
video in a smaller video theater. Were that not enough,
it hosts events and film festivals throughout the year.
✉ **1517 W Fullerton**

**Ave, Lincoln Park**
☎ **773-218-4114**
Ⓞ **Fullerton** 🚌 **74** ⚤

**Landmark 5** (4, D3)
Landmark is a chain with a
brain, a group of art-house
theaters that has updated
the package while retain-
ing the critical content,
screening a large choice of
small films from anywhere
and everywhere. The seven
small screens here draw
people who care about
films from all over town.
✉ **2828 N Clark St, Lakeview** ☎ **773-248-7744**
🅔 **www.landmarkthe
aters.com** Ⓞ **Diversey**
🚌 **22, 36, 76** ⚤

**Loews Cineplex
Entertainment 900 N
Michigan** (5, E6)
Two large (325-seat) the-
aters in the basement
under Bloomingdale's,
showing first-run features
that tend to play to the
sense and sensibility of the

Gold Coast crowd up the
block, as do policies that
bar children under five from
the theaters after 6pm.
✉ **900 N Michigan
Ave, Near North**
☎ **312-787-1988**
🅔 **www.loewscineplex
.com** Ⓞ **Chicago (Red)**
🚌 **145, 146, 147, 151**
⚤ **no children under 5
after 6pm**

**Music Box Theater**
(4, B1) This art-house
theater is a work of art in
itself, a palace from 1929
complete with organ and
machinery to make the
clouds go across the night
sky of the ceiling. It hosts
film festivals and midnight
movies, efforts worthy of
its spaces.
✉ **3733 N Southport
Ave, Lakeview West/
Southport** ☎ **773-871-
6604** 🅔 **www.music
boxtheater.com**
Ⓞ **Addison, Southport**
🚌 **152** ⚤

## Navy Pier Imax I

(5, G10) It's not every day you can see a big Hollywood movie on an enormous IMAX screen 60ft x 80ft. You can also see special 3-D IMAX productions, if only to check out the special glasses with Personal Sound Environmental Digital Sound.
✉ Navy Pier, 700 E Grand Ave, Near North ☎ 312-595-0090
e www.loewscineplex .com 🚌 124 express; 29, 56, 65, 66; 120 & 121 rush hrs only, free trolley from Grand St El station & cnr State & Rush Sts ♿

## Pipers Alley (5, A4)

This entertainment complex, opened in 1991, features four modern screening rooms that show first-run features (heavy on the indie films), and three spaces for live theater including the home of Second City's second company.
✉ 1608 N Wells St, Old Town ☎ 312-642-7500
e www.loewscineplex .com 🚇 Sedgwick 🚌 72, 156 ♿

## Gene Siskel Film Center (5, J5)

The Art Institute's film center is named for Gene

Siskel, late critic for the *Chicago Tribune*. Like other wings of the Art Institute, it aims to educate while it entertains with current and classic films that illuminate different aspects of the art and craft of movie-making.
✉ 164 N State St, The Loop ☎ 312-443-3737
e www.artic.edu
🚇 Lake/Washington
🚌 6, 29, 36, 62, 146 ♿

## Three Penny Cinema

(4, E3) For decades this tiny Lincoln Park spot has served up second-run flicks and the occasional first-run picture, usually art films but sometimes not, for bargain prices. The two

screening rooms inside are tiny but the views are unobstructed.
✉ 2424 N Lincoln Ave, Lincoln Park ☎ 773-525-2449 🚇 Fullerton
🚌 8, 11, 74 ♿

## Village Theater (5, A4)

The four screens of the Village Theater show everything from first-run flicks to foreign flicks to midnight movies. See the latest from the underground when it hosts the Chicago Underground Film Festival in summer.
✉ 1548 N Clark St, Old Town ☎ 312-642-2403
🚇 Clark/Division, Sedgwick 🚌 22, 36, 156 ♿

# THEATER & COMEDY

## About Face Theater Company (4, C3)

This company presents stories that touch or highlight gay and lesbian lives, such as the recent production of *Bash* by Chicago's Neil LaBute (author of *Your Friends and Neighbors* and *In the Company of Men*) and *Xena Live!*.
✉ 3212 N Broadway,

Lakeview ☎ 773-549-7943 e www .aboutfacetheater.com
🚇 Belmont 🚌 36, 77

## Chicago Shakespeare Company (5, G10)

The CSC presents classic Shakespeare, short Shakespeare (a *Romeo and Juliet* in 75 minutes) and other English theater clas-

sics such as Sheridan's *School for Scandal* in a stunning main theater based on the design of the Swan Theater in Stratford and a studio space for smaller shows.
✉ Navy Pier, 700 E Grand Ave, Near North ☎ 312-595-5600
e www.chicagoshakes .com 🚌 124 express;

29, 56, 65, 66; 120 & 121 rush hrs only, free trolley from Grand St El station & cnr State & Rush Sts ♿

## ComedySportz (4, D3)

As they say themselves, it's improv comedy with a competitive edge, two teams competing to do their best songs and sketches based on the suggestions from the audience. A cross of touch football and contact humor perfect for a sports crazy, comedy crazy town.
✉ 2851 N Halsted St, Lakeview ☎ 773-549-8080 e www.come dysportzchicago.com
Ⓓ Diversey 🚌 8, 22, 76

## Court Theatre (7, D4)

A repertory company based at the University of Chicago that began with a mission to present the classics of Moliere to Chekhov with a contemporary attitude, and now presents a mix of classics and contemporary work.
✉ 5535 S Ellis Ave, Hyde Park
☎ 773-753-4472
e http://courttheatre .uchicago.edu
🚌 55th-56th-57th St ♿

## Goodman Theatre

(5, J5) The oldest resident theater company in Chicago, formed in 1925 as a unit of the Art Institute, and now an independent nonprofit organization with a repertory company, a drama school and a resident production group operating from grand new quarters in The Loop.
✉ 170 N Dearborn St, The Loop ☎ 312-443-3800 e www .goodman-theatre.org
Ⓓ Clark, State 🚌 22, 36 ♿

## Second City (5, A4)

The most famous comedy troupe in America, both for age (it's been running since 1959) and even more for content, having created improv as we know it today. Most famous of all for alumni like Nichols & May and Stiller & Meara. Still running strong with shows like *Slaughterhouse 5*, *Cattle 0*.
✉ 1616 N Wells St, Old Town ☎ 312-337-3992
e www.secondcity.com
Ⓓ Sedgwick 🚌 72 ♿

## Steppenwolf Theater Company (4, G3)

An actor's theater company. In the 25 years since Steppenwolf began in a church basement in Highland Park, it's given the world such actors as Gary Sinise, Joan Allen, John Mahoney, Martha Plimpton and John Malkovich, in new works like *True West* and classics like *David Copperfield*.
✉ 1650 N Halsted St, Old Town ☎ 312-335-1650 e www .steppenwolf.org
Ⓓ North/Clybourn
🚌 8, 72 ♿

## Theater Building

(4, C2) Home base of the Famous Door Theater Company, which usually has something running on one of its three stages. Recent productions include heavy stuff from Harold Pinter and lighter stuff drawn from local life like *Hellcab* (vignettes from a cabdriver's day) and *Early and Often* (an election day comedy).
✉ 1225 W Belmont Ave, Lakeview ☎ 773-327-5252 Ⓓ Belmont
🚌 22, 77 ♿

## Victory Gardens Theater (4, E3)

An incubator of new work that calls itself, with some reason, America's Center for New Plays. There's one stage where the VGT people mount their own productions, featuring actors like Julie Harris and writers like Douglas Post, and three other stages where other companies present equally edgy performances.
✉ 2257 N Lincoln Ave, Lincoln Park ☎ 773-871-3000 e www .victorygardens.org
Ⓓ Fullerton
🚌 8, 11, 22, 36 ♿

## WNEP Theater (4, C3)

This intimate neighborhood theater hosts a smorgasbord of shows over the course of any week ranging from comedy performance act (the 'Soiree Dada,' in the original faux-German) to performance art (did they say 'kung fu musical?').
✉ 3209 N Halsted St, Lakeview
☎ 773-755-1693
Ⓓ Belmont 🚌 8, 77

Raymond Hillstrom

*Good Old Goodman*

# GAY & LESBIAN CHICAGO

Most gay clubs are on Halsted St between Belmont Ave (3200 N) and Grace St (3800 N). If you don't see what you're looking for in the listings, get out there and look for yourself. Further info for gay and lesbian travelers on p. 119.

**Berlin** (4, C2)
A dance club with special events from Testosterone Tuesdays to Women's Obsession (on Wed) to Prince Nights (as in artist-formerly …), all offering proof that sexual orientation is a very broad continuum.
✉ **954 W Belmont Ave, Lakeview** ☎ 773-348-4975 ⊕ **Belmont** 🚌 **8, 22, 77** ⏰ **Mon 8pm-4am, Tues-Fri 5pm-4am, Sat 6pm-5am, Sun 6pm-4am**

**Chicago Eagle** (3, B7)
Any bar that you enter through the back of a semi-truck can't be all bad, if you're looking to be bad in the first place. Get your boots shined upstairs, or take a shine to a stranger in the Pit downstairs
✉ **5015 N Clark St, Andersonville** ☎ 773-728-0050 ⊕ **Argyle** 🚌 **22** ⏰ **Sun-Thurs 8pm-4am, Sat 8pm-5am**

**Circuit** (4, B3)
Circuit has one of the biggest dance bars in Boystown downstairs, and smaller (if not necessarily

intimate) bars upstairs. The perfect place to look for shirtless boys on whatever, dancing like extras from an episode of 'Queer as Folk.'
✉ **3641 N Halsted St, Wrigleyville** ☎ 773-325-2233 ⊕ **Addison** 🚌 **8, 152** ⏰ **Wed-Thurs 9pm-2am, Fri & Sun 9pm-4am, Sat 9pm-5am**

**Cocktail** (4, C3)
This is the hippest neighborhood bar in Boystown. Sleek yet still unpretentious, quiet enough to chat in the front room and loud enough to dance in the back room. Popular with lesbians Mon and the martini set Tues when it's Rat Pack night.
✉ **3359 N Halsted St, Lakeview** ☎ 773-477-1420 ⊕ **Belmont** 🚌 **8** ⏰ **Mon-Fri 4pm-2am, Sat 4pm-3am, Sun 2pm-2am**

**Gentry of Chicago** (5, H5) A change of pace from the disco and denim of Boystown, Gentry has a piano bar and quiet spaces in its new location in the Near North (a few blocks

south of its original spot on Rush St) and uptown amid the commotion (4, B3; 3320 N Halsted St).
✉ **440 N State St, Near North** ☎ 312-664-1033 ⊕ **Grand** 🚌 **22, 36** ⏰ **Sun-Fri 4pm-2am, Sat 4pm-3am**

**Manhole** (4, B3)
A bar and dance club for the leather and muscle set. The doors open at 9pm but don't even think about coming until close to midnight. A strict dress code applies on weekends; you'll need to be shirtless or in leather.
✉ **3458 N Halsted St, Wrigleyville** ☎ 773-975-9244 ⊕ **Addison** 🚌 **8** ⏰ **Sun-Fri 9pm-4am, Sat 9pm-5am**

**SideTrack** (4, C3)
If you're looking for very cute, very well-dressed lads, look no further than the SideTrack. Leave your BMW with the valet outside, check in your Banana Republic jacket with the cloakroom inside and have a good time.
✉ **3349 N Halsted St, Lakeview** ☎ 773-477-9189 ⊕ **Belmont** 🚌 **8** ⏰ **Mon-Fri 3pm-2am, Sat 2pm-3am, Sun 2pm-2am**

**Roscoe's** (4, C3)
The Great America of gay nightlife, with three bars, a dance floor and a couple of extra rooms in between. There's even an outside patio weather permitting. Great for a drink on weeknights, or a dance and maybe a different kind of

## Go, Girls
There's a decent range of lesbian nightlife in Chicago. **Girlbar** (4, D3; 2625 N Halsted St; ☎ 773-871-4210) is a place to hang out and perhaps make a new friend. **The Closet** (4, C3; 3325 N Broadway; ☎ 773-477-8533) is lesbian-owned and filled with a mix of lesbians, gay men and friendly straights. For other dancing options, **Berlin** (p. 94) hosts **Women's Obsession** Wed, and **Star Gaze** in Andersonville (3, B7; 5419 N Clark St; ☎ 773-561-7363) plays retro Thursday, salsa Friday and contemporary sounds Saturday.

pick-me-up on weekends.
✉ 3356 N Halsted St, Wrigleyville
☎ 773-281-3355
🕐 Addison 🚌 8
🕐 Mon-Thurs 2pm-2am, Fri 1pm-2am, Sat noon-3am, Sun noon-2am

**Voltaire** (4, B3)
For those of you who thought cabaret was dead, guess again. This supper club presents reviews five nights a week featuring performers who can really sing and dance and kid with the audience, vivid examples of the city's vast pool of talent.
✉ 3441 N Halsted St, Wrigleyville ☎ 773-281-9320 🕐 Addison 🚌 8 🕐 Mon-Fri 3pm-2am, Sat 3pm-3am, Sun 11am-2am

# CLASSICAL MUSIC, DANCE & OPERA

### Chicago Symphony Orchestra (5, L6)
A local institution whose international reputation consistently rivals the Art Institute's. Start with a site on Michigan Ave facing Grant Park, add an auditorium with astounding acoustics, fill it with talented musicians, top them with a world-famous conductor and you have a recipe for success for over 50 years.
✉ Orchestra Hall, 220 S Michigan Ave, The Loop ☎ 312-294-3000
e www.chicagosymphony.org 🕐 Adams, Jackson 🚌 1, 3, 4, 6, 145, 146, 147, 151 ♿

### Hubbard Street Dance Chicago (5, K4)
Hubbard Street Dance Chicago is a first-rate modern dance troupe, the only serious game in town until the Joffrey arrived in the mid-1990s, one well watching whatever your options. It's graduated from Hubbard St to a permanent home in the West Loop and performances at the Cadillac Palace downtown.
✉ Cadillac Palace Theater, 151 W Randolph St, The Loop
☎ 312-850-9744
e www.hubbardstreetdance.com
🕐 Clark, Washington (Brown) 🚌 156

### Ravinia
Some of the best places to hear music around Chicago are under the stars, and the best open-air music is at Ravinia in suburban Highland Park (1, B3; on Green Bay Rd, a ½-mile north of Lake-Cook Rd; ☎ 847-266-5100). The Chicago Symphony plays a couple of times a week in season and jazz and pop artists fill in the rest of the schedule. If the music really matters to you, try to get reserved seats in the covered pavilion where the acoustics and sightlines are good. If you care more about the stars above, pack a hamper for a picnic on the lawn.

### Joffrey Ballet (5, M6)
Robert Joffrey created a company and a name for himself starting with classic ballet dancing, beautifully executed, then playing with classic forms to create original work with a pop art sensibility. The company moved here in the 1990s, where it performs at the Auditorium Building and Ravinia.
✉ Auditorium Bldg, 50 E Congress Pkwy, Grant Park ☎ 312-739-0120
e www.joffrey.com
🕐 Library, Harrison 🚇 Van Buren 🚌 6, 146

### Lyric Opera of Chicago (5, K3)
A solid company with a solid reputation, Lyric Opera presents a mix of the stand-bys and the new. Its immense (3500-seat) theater is a 1920s masterpiece tucked into a 45-story limestone tower, built by utilities magnate Samuel Insull to rival the Auditorium Building.
✉ Civic Opera House, 20 N Wacker Dr, The Loop ☎ 312-332-2244
e www.lyricopera.org
🕐 Washington (Brown) 🚌 157

Richard l'Anson

*Do the Cadillac walk, leap, pirouette...*

# JAZZ, BLUES & FOLK

**The Blue Note** (2, D4)
Look for the single blue note on the front door to find the only place in Wicker Park that presents live music that's not rock or a derivative. You'll find jazz, blues, big band and swing and occasional trips into acid jazz, salsa or R & B.
✉ **1565 N Milwaukee Ave, Wicker Park**
☎ 773-489-0011
🚇 Damen 🚌 50, 56, 72 ⏰ Sun-Fri 8pm-4am, Sat 8pm-5am

**B.L.U.E.S.** (4, D3)
A no-frills operation that's generally considered the best blues club in Chicago, as much for the ambience of the room and the crowd as for the high quality of the performers. Kingston Mines may be bigger, Buddy Guys may be fancier, but B.L.U.E.S. has that authentic juke joint feeling.
✉ **2519 N Halsted St, Lincoln Park**
☎ 773-525-8371
🚇 Fullerton 🚌 8 ⏰ Sun-Fri 8pm-2am, Sat 8pm-3am

**Buddy Guys Legends** (5, N6) The premiere blues club in town presenting some of the top names in the business seven nights a week. Don't be put off by the size of the room or the tourist/conventioneer contingent. You'll get a great show, and a great meal too (they serve soul food) if you're hungry.
✉ **754 S Wabash Ave, The Loop**
☎ 312-427-0333
e www.buddyguys.com
🚇 Harrison 🚌 6, 145, 147, 151 ⏰ Sun-Fri 5pm-2am, Sat 5pm-3am

**Green Dolphin Street** (4, E1) A jazz and supper club for adults from the people who own Café Absinthe and the Red Dog in Wicker Park. This is decidedly upscale, from the elegant dining room to the wood-paneled club. Latin and world jazz prevail, as easy on the ears as the surroundings are easy on the eyes.
✉ **2200 N Ashland Ave, Lincoln Park West**
☎ 773-395-0066
e www.jazzitup.com
🚌 9, 74 ⏰ Tues-Thurs 5.30-10pm, Fri & Sat 5.30-11pm, Sun 5.30-10pm

**Green Mill** (3, B7)
An Uptown club that dates back to Prohibition, presenting a mix of regulars and visiting acts from big band sounds to atonal stuff. Try swing dancing Tues or Thurs or the Uptown Poetry Slam Sun 7-10pm.
✉ **4802 N Broadway, Uptown**
☎ 773-878-5552
🚇 Lawrence 🚌 36 ⏰ Mon-Fri noon-4am, Sat noon-5am, Sun 11am-4am

**Jazz Showcase** (5, G5)
A classic case of truth in advertising. Joe Segal has been showcasing the best jazz performers in the world since his days as a student at Roosevelt University. His Near North spot is part club, part classroom (there's a kid-friendly matinee Sun). A little dressy so be prepared.
✉ **59 W Grand Ave, Near North** ☎ 312-670-2473 🚇 Grand 🚌 22, 36, 65 ⏰ shows Tues-Thurs 8pm & 10pm, Fri & Sat 9pm & 11pm, Sun 4pm, 8pm & 10pm ♿ special shows for children Sun 4pm

*Just singin' the blues...*

**Kingston Mines** (4, D3)
For over 30 years, Kingston Mines has served up the blues from two stages to tourists and locals and an after-hours crowd (this is the only blues club in the town with a 4am license). The music starts at 9.30pm and runs to closing every night.
✉ **2548 N Halsted St, Lincoln Park**
☎ 773-477-4646
e www.kingston-mines.com 🚇 Fullerton 🚌 8 ⏰ Sun-Fri 8pm-4am, Sat 8pm-5am

**Old Town School of Folk Music** (3, B7)
The new uptown headquarters of the Old Town School presents folk, country and bluegrass concerts most weekends in its 420-seat theater. Hear anyone from Tom Rush to Tish Hinojosa depending on your luck and the whim of the booking department.
✉ **4544 N Lincoln Ave, Ravenswood** ☎ 773-728-6000 🚇 Western (Brown) 🚌 11 ⏰ box office Mon-Thurs 9.30am-10pm, Fri & Sat 9.30am-5pm ♿

# ROCK, ALTERNATIVE & WORLD MUSIC

### The Aragon Ballroom

(3, B7) This place was built in 1926 as a courtyard in Spain for 4500 dancers. Ballroom dancing is out now and the 'Brawlroom' is in, with signs that say 'No Stage Dancing, Body Surfing' as the place hosts acts like Alanis Morissette and Paul Oakenfield or big Latin dance parties (ole!)
✉ 1106 W Lawrence Ave, Uptown ☎ 773-561-9500 Ⓣ Lawrence 🚌 36

### Double Door (2, D4)

The Goldilocks rock club – not too little, not too big, just the right size – run by the same people who run the Metro, an anchor of the Bucktown/Wicker Park scene. Just about every kind of live music this side of jazz, so call before you go unless you're willing to be surprised.
✉ 1572 N Milwaukee Ave, Wicker Park ☎ 773-489-3160 Ⓣ Damen 🚌 50, 56, 72

### Elbo Room (4, D2)

Live music with no frills and minimal attitude. There's no cover charge to hang in the cozy bar on the ground floor, a low cover charge to go downstairs to see and hear the (usually) local working rawest facet of modern music from rock to reggae to hip hop to ska.
✉ 2871 N Lincoln Ave, Lakeview ☎ 773-549-5549 Ⓣ Diversey 🚌 11, 76

### HotHouse (5, N6)

The hottest spot for world music and jazz, a nonprofit club with two smallish spaces dedicated to presenting music and performances from around the country.

Call ahead to confirm what's on the cultural menu.
✉ 31 E Balbo Dr, The Loop ☎ 312-362-9707 Ⓣ Harrison 🚌 6, 145, 147, 151 ⚤ under 21 generally admitted

### House of Blues (5, H5)

This is not a misprint. House of Blues is listed here because it presents rock and soul and world music groups, big-name acts in a big venue (1500 seats, sky-boxes and all). It's an eclectic booking policy (the proverbial big tent), so you might even hear the blues.
✉ 329 N Dearborn St, Near North
☎ 312-923-2000 Ⓣ State, Lake 🚌 22, 36

### The Metro (4, B2)

This is the Big Kahuna of the live music scene, a converted movie theater that holds about 1100 people. Thousands of acts have played here, from Nirvana to Bob Dylan to Megadeth. Worth checking the schedule any night of the week.
✉ 3730 N Clark St, Wrigleyville
☎ 773-549-3604 Ⓣ Addison 🚌 22, 152

### Schubas Tavern & Harmony Grill (4, C1)

Schubas may be the hardest place in town to categorize,

surpassing House of Blues. It came to attention with alternative country. Now you can hear anything from Aussie country to Goth rock to bluegrass. Microbrews on tap and great food at the grill.
✉ 3159 Southport Ave, Lakeview West/ Southport ☎ 773-525-25-8 Ⓣ Belmont 🚌 77

### The Vic (4, C2)

When this old movie theater isn't presenting flicks with suds as the Brew & View it's hosting live music from national acts to locals, from folk rock to the head-bashing stuff.
✉ 3145 N Sheffield St, Lakeview ☎ 773-472-0366 Ⓣ Belmont 🚌 22, 72 ⚤ under 21 generally admitted

### The Wild Hare (4, B2)

This looks like a dive from the outside, but inside the Wild Hare is the reggae capital of America. The facilities are first-rate. The acts are world-class whether local or imported. The ambience is top-flight whether you're dancing in back or hanging in front.
✉ 3530 N Clark St, Wrigleyville ☎ 773-327-4273 Ⓣ Addison 🚌 22, 152 🕐 Sun-Fri 8pm-2am, Sat 8pm-3am

### Petrillo Music Shell

From June through August, the Petrillo Music Shell (5, L7; S Columbus Dr at E Jackson Blvd, ☎ 312-744-3315) in Grant Park hosts one festival after another, including the Gospel Festival, the Blues Festival, the Country Music Festival, a Latin music festival, the Jazz Festival and the Celtic Festival. For more details check the Web site at Ⓔ www.ci.chi.il.us/SpecialEvents/Festivals.

# SPECTATOR SPORT

Until Michael Jordan came along, Chicago was largely known for second-rate (or worse) teams. Perennial failure didn't dampen local interest, but the long reign of the Bulls has made Chicagoans less defensive about their teams.

## Baseball

Chicago has two major league baseball teams, the **Chicago Cubs** of the National League and the **Chicago White Sox** of the American League. The Cubs are far and away better known although they last won a World Series in 1908 and last played in the World Series in 1945. They may not field winning teams, but their field is the best in the business. Wrigley (p. 29) is old (built in 1914) and old-fashioned (they installed lights for night baseball in 1988). It's accessible, next to the Addison El station in one of the nicer neighborhoods of the North Side, with direct access from anywhere along the lakefront between The Loop and suburban Wilmette.

### Gambling
There are 'riverboat' casinos that work the Fox River in the far western suburbs and other 'riverboat' casinos in the old mill towns along the Indiana shore. Try your luck at the **Grand Casino Victoria**, in Elgin (1, D1; 250 S Grove Ave; ☎ 847-888-1000), the **Trump Casino Boat** in Gary (1, E4; 1 Buffington Harbor Dr; ☎ 888-218-7867) or the **Majestic Star Casino Boat** next door (1, E4; 1 Buffington Harbor Dr; ☎ 219-977-7777).

The Sox have their fans, despite their location near some of the worst slums on the Near South Side (many of which are coming down), and their new stadium, **Comiskey Park** (3, F8; 333 W 35th St; ☎ 312-674-1000), generally considered the least interesting ballpark built in North America in recent years. The Sox have a much better record than the Cubs, though they're best known for the Black Sox team in 1919 that threw the World Series to the Cincinnati Red. (If you're interested, rent *Field of Dreams* at the local video store for an entertaining twist on the Black Sox story).

## Basketball

Basketball now matches baseball as Chicago's favorite spectator sport. Since Michael Jordan retired for the second time in 1997, the **Chicago Bulls** are a shadow of their former selves and it is possible to get tickets to games at the **United Center Arena** (3, E7; 1901 W Madison St; ☎ 312-455-4000) on the Near West Side.

*If you close your eyes you can still see Michael.*

# Football

The **Chicago Bears** are cousins of the Cubs. Built by owner-coach George Hallas in the early days of the National Football League, when players were working guys who loved the game, the team used to play in the Friendly Confines before moving to the much-bigger Soldier Field at the south end of Grant Park in the 1960s.

*Bears practise manoeuvres at Soldiers Field.*

Their record was better than the Cubs, to be fair, though they only went to the Super Bowl once (in 1986). Players like Walter Payton, Jim McMahon and William 'the Refrigerator' Perry working under coaches like Hallas and Mike Ditka have given Bears fans enough action to keep them coming back for more.

The **Northwestern Wildcats** host other Big-Ten teams at Ryan Stadium (1, C3; 1501 Central Ave; ☎ 847-491-2287) near the Evanston campus, a short walk from the Central El station on the Purple Line (Northwestern colors are purple and white). They had a great run in the mid-1990s, going all the way to the Rose Bowl in 1995, but lately they've been back to their role as the Cubs of Midwest football.

# Ice Hockey

The **Chicago Blackhawks** were one of the original US members of the National Hockey League, before expansion fever took teams to sunbelt cities like Atlanta and Anaheim. They never made much of a splash aside from a rivalry with the Detroit Red Wings, which has somehow managed to fire up fans year after year. They also play at **United Center Arena** (3, E7; 1901 W Madison St; ☎ 312-455-7000)

# Horse Racing

The **Arlington International Racecourse** in the northwestern suburb of Arlington Heights (1, B1; 2200 W Euclid Ave, Arlington Hts; ☎ 847-255-4300; Northwest Metra line, Arlington Park station) is the upmarket track in the area. The season runs May to September. **Sportsman's Park** on the West Side near Midway Airport (3, F5; 3301 S Laramie Ave, Cicero; ☎ 773-242-1121; Aurora Metra line, Cicero Ave sta-

*Race out to Arlington for some track action.*

tion) is the working guy's track. It's been remodeled to accommodate auto racing and horse racing. Horse racing runs March to mid-May.

# places to stay

Since the railroads arrived in the 1850s, Chicago has been filled with travelers and hotels for travelers to stay in. Some merely stopped to rest while changing trains, others came to do business, still others to attend meetings or conventions.

The business focus of the hotel business survives to this day. There are over 28,000 rooms inside city limits, and thousands more under construction, most in large convention hotels or expense-account palazzi. It's a mixed blessing. What you lose in charm you often gain in service and facilities. Not every hotel is a behemoth. There are mid-sized properties from the 1920s on the Gold Coast and the Near North Side, small rehabbed properties from the 1990s, and a handful of tiny hotels and motels scattered across the North Side.

### Room Rates

The price ranges in this chapter indicate the cost of a standard double room.

| | |
|---|---|
| Deluxe | from $300 |
| Top End | $200-299 |
| Mid-Range | $100-199 |
| Budget | under $100 |

Tom Given

Whatever your choice, book as early as possible. From 1994 to 2000 occupancy rates rose from 67.9% to 74.2%. This includes January and February, so there will be times that even Richard M. Daley himself will have trouble finding a room at the inn.

## Booking Agents

Booking agents or service bureaus can often get you into a mid-range or top-end hotel that is otherwise fully committed. The **Illinois Reservation Service** (☎ 1-800-491-1800) will help you hunt for a room free of charge. There may be a booking charge if you cancel, depending on the policy of the hotel involved. **Hot Rooms** (☎ 1-800-468-3500, 773-468-7666; [e] www.hotrooms.com) can help you find rooms at 25 properties in town, often at a discount from the rack rates. If you cancel, you will be charged a $25 fee. **Bed & Breakfast Chicago** (☎ 1-800-375-7084, 773-248-0005; [e] www.chicago-bed-break fast.com) owns and operates a B&B in Lincoln Park and represents other B&Bs around town.

### Big Spaces

The City of the Big Shoulders is also the City of the Big Hotels. The Hilton & Towers on S Michigan Ave was the largest hotel in the world for decades. Slimmed down to a mere 1543 guest spaces, it no longer holds the title even for Chicago. The Palmer House Hilton, below, nearby has 1693 rooms, not enough to match the Hyatt Regency Chicago on E Wacker Dr which weighs in with 2019 rooms.

# DELUXE

### The Drake (5, D6)
The queen of the Magnificent Mile sits at the top of Michigan Ave, overlooking the Oak St Beach and the lakefront, as far as the eye can see. The view inside is equally grand, with imposing public rooms and concourses below, and elegant guest rooms above.
✉ 140 E Walton St at Michigan Ave, Near North ☎ 312-787-2200, 1-800-553-7253; fax 312-787-1431
e www.thedrake hotel.com ⊙ Chicago (Red) 🚌 145, 146, 147, 151 ✕ Cape Cod Room

### Four Seasons (5, E6)
When you arrive at the sky lobby it's hard to believe you're in a tower hundreds of feet above the Magnificent Mile. Fires in fireplaces, fine rugs on marble floors, and traditional furniture in the lobbies and rooms create an effect that's as 1890 as the views that scream '1990'.
✉120 E Delaware Pl at Michigan Ave, Near North ☎ 312-280-8800, 1-800-332-3442; fax 312-280-9184
e www.fourseasons .com ⊙ Chicago (Red) 🚌 145, 146, 147, 151 ✕ Seasons

### Ritz-Carlton Chicago
(5, E6) This was one of the first modern luxury hotels on the Near North Side and it's still one of the best, from the exquisite service to the exquisite facilities including an indoor pool with a view from halfway up Water Tower Place.
✉160 E Pearson St at Michigan Ave, Near North ☎ 312-266-1000, 1-800-621-6906; fax 312-266-9498
e www.fourseasons .com ⊙ Chicago (Red) 🚌 145, 146, 147, 151 ✕ The Café

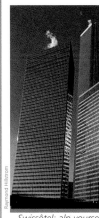

*Swissôtel: alp yourself to a view*

### Swissôtel (5, H7)
Everyone has a view of the river or the lake or the city from this sleek triangular tower in the Illinois Center. This is a favorite with business travelers because of the location and a favorite of pleasure travelers because of the weekend package rates.
✉ 323 E Wacker Dr, The Loop ☎ 312-565-0565, 1-800-637-9477; fax 312-565-0540
e www.swissotel.com ⊙ State, Lake 🚆 Randolph 🚌 4, 6, 56 ✕ Café Suisse

### Sutton Place (5, D5)
A Eurostylish property from the 1980s just right for its location around the corner from the best Oak St boutiques. Look for photographs of flowers by Robert Mapplethorpe in the guest rooms, alongside individual stereo systems and baths with separate tubs and showers.
✉ 21 E Bellevue St, Gold Coast ☎ 312-266-2100, 1-800-606-8186; fax 312-266-2141
e www.suttonplace .com ⊙ Clark/Division 🚌 36, 151, 152 ✕ The Whiskey

### The Tremont (5, E6)
The Tremont is a more casual version of the Whitehall around the corner, a residential building that's now a hotel with a residential feeling. Some of the rooms may come in funny shapes and sizes, but all come fully equipped with modern gadgetry backed by traditional service and staff.
✉ 100 E Chestnut St, Near North ☎ 312-751-1900, 1-800-621-8133; fax 312-751-8691
⊙ Chicago (Red) 🚌 145, 146, 147, 151 ✕ Iron Mike's Grill

### Whitehall Hotel (5, E6)
The Whitehall was built as a luxury apartment building in the 1920s and converted into a luxury hotel in the 70s. It still feels residential (there are only 221 rooms) which accounts for its appeal to tycoons and the like.
✉ 105 E Delaware Pl, Near North ☎ 312-944-6300, 1-800-948-4255; fax 312-944-8522
⊙ Chicago (Red) 🚌 145, 146, 147, 151 ✕ Whitehall Place

Raymond Hillstrom

# TOP END

## Ambassador East
(5, B5) This Gold Coast landmark was built in the 1920s as a mate to the Ambassador West across the street. A celebrity hangout in years gone by, it's famous for its supporting role in the film *North by Northwest* and for the star-studded guest list at the Pump Room (now, largely a thing of the past).
✉ 1301 N State St, Gold Coast ☎ 312-787-7200, 1-800-843-6664; fax 312-787-4760
ⓔ www.omnihotels.com
Ⓜ Clark/Division 🚌 22, 36 ✕ Pump Room

## Chicago Hilton & Towers
(5, N6)
For years, this was the largest hotel in the world. It's still a monster, with 1500 rooms sprawling over a full city block. The rooms have been recently refurbished and modern amenities like an indoor lap pool, a sun deck and a free shuttle to the Water Tower add to the package.
✉ 720 S Michigan Ave, The Loop ☎ 312-922-4400, 1-800-445-8667; fax 312-922-5240
ⓔ www.hilton.com
Ⓜ Harrison
🚆 Roosevelt 🚌 1, 3, 4, 6
✕ The Pavilion

*Nouveau plush rules at Hotel Allegro.*

## Doubletree Guest Suites
(5, E7)
A modern all-suites property that's about to get a facelift from its new corporate owners to gear it even more to business travelers. You'll find the nicely configured rooms and the modest pool and fitness facilities that you'd expect from Doubletree.
✉ 198 E Delaware Pl, Near North ☎ 312-664-1100, 1-800-424-2900; fax 312-664-9881
ⓔ www.doubletree.com
Ⓜ Chicago (Red)
🚌 145, 146, 147, 151
✕ Mrs Park's Tavern

## Hotel Allegro
(5, K4)
Music swirls around you, in the air and on walls, as you step in from the sidewalk on The Loop's Theater Row and up the stairs into the nouveau-plush lobby. The rooms also are nouveau-plush, and inviting, as at its sister hotels, the Burnham and the Monaco.
✉ 171 W Randolph St, The Loop ☎ 312-236-0123, 1-800-643-1500; fax 312-236-3440
ⓔ www.allegrochicago.com Ⓜ Clark, Washington
🚌 6, 29, 36, 62, 146
✕ 312 Chicago Café

## Hotel Burnham
(5, K5)
This classic Chicago Style office building was designed by Burnham & Root in 1895, designated a National Historic Landmark about 100 years later and gracefully converted to a 120-room hotel. Original woodwork, tilework and cast iron detailing in the hallways conceal cozy modern rooms with sensational views.
✉ 1 W Washington Blvd, The Loop

## The Usual Suspects
All the big US hotel chains have properties in Chicago. In addition to the chain hotels listed in this chapter, you can find **Holiday Inns** (☎ 1-800-445-8667), more **Hiltons** (☎ 1-800-445-8667), two **Hyatt Regencies** (☎ 1-800-233-1234), a **Westin**, at right, (☎ 1-800-228-3000), a **Wyndham** (☎ 1-800-996-3426) and a couple of **Marriotts** (☎ 1-800-228-9290).

☎ 312-782-1111, 877-294-9712; fax 312-782-0899 **e** www.burnham hotel.com ⊕ Washington 🚍 6, 29, 36, 62, 146 ✕ Atwood Café (p. 78)

### Hotel Inter-Continental (5, G6)

The south half of the Intercon was built as the Medinah Men's Athletic Club in 1929, which accounts for one of the nicest swimming pools this side of San Simeon. There's a massive renovation under way that will reconfigure the lobby and refurbish the south tower rooms.

✉ 505 N Michigan Ave, Near North ☎ 312-944-4100; fax 312-944-3050 **e** www.chicago.inter conti.com ⊕ Grand 🚍 145, 146, 147, 151 ✕ Amber

### Hotel Monaco (5, J6)

The sister hotel to the Allegro and the Burnham, the Monaco features the same warm decor in the lobby and guest rooms, the same contemporary American cooking in the restaurant and the same friendly competent service.

✉ 225 N Wabash Ave, The Loop ☎ 312-960-8500; fax 312-960-8538 **e** www.monaco-chica go.com ⊕ State, Lake 🚆 Randolph 🚍 6, 36, 145, 146, 147, 151 ✕ Mossant Bistro

### House of Blues (5, H5)

Across from the HOB nightclub, just above a bowling alley and a Crunch fitness facility, the House of Blues Hotel is for people with entertainment on their minds. The rooms are bright enough to suggest a need for sunglasses. The

lobby is dark enough to suggest Rick's quarters in *Casablanca*.

✉ 333 N Dearborn St at the River, Near North ☎ 312-245-0333, 877-569-3742; fax 312-923-2444 **e** www.loews hotels.com ⊕ State, Lake 🚍 29, 36, 62 ✕ Smith & Wollensky

### Lenox Suites Hotel

(5, G6) Over 300 suites in five different configurations in a great location behind the Magnificent Mile and across from the 600 N Michigan Cineplex and a branch of Heaven on Seven. Cheerful decor and kitchenettes with real appliances (dishes and cookware available on request) fill out the package.

✉ 616 N Rush St, Near North ☎ 312-337-1000, 1-800-445-3669; fax 312-337-7217 **e** www.lenoxsuites.com ⊕ Grand 🚍 3, 145, 146, 147, 151 ✕ Houston's

### Raphael (5, E7)

This was one of the first small European-style hotels in town, opened in the late 1970s. It was a winning formula, attracting a loyal clientele to this Near North residential block. The rooms could use a little fluffing, but it continues to offer good value in a great location.

✉ 201 E Delaware Pl, Near North ☎ 312-943-5000; fax 312-943-5480 ⊕ Chicago (Red) 🚍 145, 146, 147, 151 ✕ Park Avenue Café

### Seneca (5, E7)

Half the suites in this apartment hotel are occupied by long-term residents. Travelers on short stays will

enjoy the residential feel and the residential amenities of the suites, such as full kitchenettes, in-house fitness room, beauty parlor and roof deck. One of the better deals in town.

✉ 200 E Chestnut St, Near North ☎ 312-787-8900, 1-800-800-6261; fax 312-988-4438 **e** www.senecahotel. com ⊕ Chicago (Red) 🚍 145, 146, 147, 151 ✕ Chalfin's Delicatessen & The Saloon

### Sheraton (5, H7)

If you have to stay in a big convention hotel, make it this one. The rooms face the river and The Loop, making for glorious views, and the location behind the Tribune Tower and the NBC Building is a great base camp for assaults on The Loop or the Magnificent Mile.

✉ 301 N Water St, Near North ☎ 312-464-1000, 877-242-2558; fax 312-464-9140 **e** www.sheraton.com ⊕ Grand 🚍 145, 146, 147, 151 ✕ Riverside Café

*Expect some royal treatment at Hotel Monaco.*

# MID-RANGE

### Allerton Crowne Plaza (5, F6)
Don't let the lobby or the Crowne Plaza label put you off. This 1920s Michigan Ave landmark was gracefully and thoroughly renovated in the 1990s. The rooms are warm and plush, not the least bit 'chain hotel' feeling. The fitness center has a spectacular view down to The Loop.
⊠ 701 N Michigan Ave, Near North ☎ 312-440-1500, 1-800-621-8311; fax 312-440-1819
e www.bristolhotels .com ⊕ Chicago (Red) ⬚ 145, 146, 147, 151 ✕ Taps on Two

### Best Western Inn of Chicago (5, G6)
This is a cozy older hotel that was refurbished and reflagged a few years ago. At the lower end of the middle range, it's good value for a great location one block off the heart of the Mag Mile.
⊠ 162 E Ohio St, Near North ☎ 312-787-3100, 1-800-557-2378; fax 312-573-3136
e www.bestwestern .com ⊕ Grand ⬚ 145, 146, 147, 151, 157 ✕ Newsmaker Café

### Best Western River North (5, G4)
The largest motel on the LaSalle St strip was actually a cold storage warehouse, which makes sense when you look at it. The rooms are fitted with mod cons including Nintendo players and programmable safes.

Other amenities include a pool and a fitness room and free parking.
⊠ 125 W Ohio St, River North ☎ 312-467-0800; fax 312-467-1665
e www.bestwestern .com ⊕ Grand ⬚ 156 ✕ Pizzeria Ora

### Claridge (5, C5)
A sophisticated older hotel on a quiet block in the Gold Coast. As in other older properties, the rooms can vary dramatically in size and shape, so ask questions in advance if this matters to you. Three suites have working fireplaces for romantic rendezvous.
⊠ 1244 N Dearborn St, Gold Coast ☎ 312-787-4980, 1-800-245-1258; fax 312-266-0978
e www.claridgehotel .com ⊕ Clark/Division ⬚ 22, 36 ✕ Foreign Affairs

### Habitat Corporate Suites
The Habitat people rent out furnished apartments by the month in a number of high-rise buildings on the Near North Side and in the West Loop near the train stations. Avoid West Loop properties if you can, as the neighborhood is relatively inconvenient and fairly boring.
☎ 312-902-2090; fax 312-902-2070
e www.habitatcsn.com

### Radisson Hotel & Suites (5, F6)
An unassuming medium-sized (430 rooms and suites) hotel in a good Near North location between Michigan Ave and the Northwestern University

## Conventions
Chicago invented the convention business as we know it. As de Toqueville observed 150 years ago, Americans love forming associations that require them to attend lots of meetings. Chicago's central location and direct rail service to every part of the country made it the natural spot for the meeting business.

If this means you're on a trip to Chicago to attend a convention, that's great. If you're planning a pleasure trip, you might check with the **Chicago Convention and Tourism Bureau** (☎ 312-567-8000; e www.choosechicago.com) or call the reservations desk at one of the big hotels to avoid competing with thousands of happy radiologists for rooms and restaurant reservations.

Richard Cummins

campus. Check out the views from the open air pool deck on the 40th fl.
✉ 160 E Huron St, Near North ☎ 312-787-2900, 1-800-333-3333; fax 312-787-5158
e www.radisson chicago.com
⊙ Chicago (Red)
🚌 3, 145, 146, 147, 151
✗ Red Rock Grill

**Residence Inn** (5, D7)
An undistinguished apartment building improved by its conversion into a comfortable long-term stay hotel (this one by the Marriott people). You'll find a breakfast buffet downstairs and a social hour with drinks Mon-Thurs evening.
✉ 201 E Walton St, Near North ☎ 312-943-9800, 1-800-331-3131; fax 312-943-8579
e www.marriot.com
⊙ Chicago
🚌 145, 146, 147, 151
✗ Mrs Park's Tavern

**Silversmith** (5, L6)
This boutique hotel near the jeweler's buildings on Wabash Ave was built to house silversmiths in 1897 and listed on the National Register of Historic Landmarks about 100 years later. All the usual conveniences provided in a most unusual package.
✉ 10 S Wabash Ave, The Loop ☎ 312-372-7696, 1-800-227-6963; fax 312-372-7320
e www.crowneplaza .com ⊙ Madison, Monroe 🚊 Randolph
🚌 3, 4, 60, 145, 147, 151
✗ Ada's Famous Deli & Restaurant

**Summerfield Suites** (5, F6) One of two Near North apartment buildings converted into long-term stay hotels. This property offers studios, parlors and one-bedroom units all with kitchenette or microwave/ refrigerator combinations, a

rooftop pool and an exercise room. Breakfast and snacks come as part of the package.
✉ 166 E Superior St, Near North ☎ 312-787-6000, 1-800-833-4353; fax 312-787-6133
e www.summerfield suites.com ⊙ Chicago (Red) 🚌 145, 146, 147, 151
✗ The Avenue Café

**Talbott Hotel** (5, E5)
A small (149-room) European-style hotel from the 1920s with a sweet outdoor cafe facing a quiet side street on the busy Near North Side. Popular with business travelers, although you won't feel out of place walking through the lobby without a briefcase or a Palm Pilot.
✉ 20 E Delaware Pl, Near North ☎ 312-944-4970, 1-800-825-2688; fax 312-944-7241
e www.talbotthotel .com ⊙ Chicago (Red)
🚌 36 ✗ Basil's

# BUDGET

**City Suites** (4, C2)
The location on the busiest block of Belmont Ave a couple of steps from entrance to the Belmont El station, screams 'big city.' The screaming stops inside the door in a quiet lobby, where a light breakfast is served every morning, heading to restful rooms above.
✉ 933 W Belmont Ave, Lakeview/Wrigleyville ☎ 773-404-3400, 1-800-248-9108; fax 773-404-3405
e www.cityinns.com
⊙ Belmont
🚌 8, 22, 77
✗ Ann Sather (p. 74)

**Comfort Inn Lincoln Park** (4, D3)
These may be Lincoln Park's least expensive hotel rooms with private baths for all. Seventy-four cozy rooms, all recently refurbished, with the usual conveniences such as phones and cable TV, just off the busiest corner in the neighborhood. Cheap parking tops off the bargain.
✉ 601 W Diversey Pkwy, Lincoln Park ☎ 773-348-2810, 1-800-228-5100; fax 773-348-1912 e www.comfort inn.com ⊙ Diversey
🚌 22, 36 ✗ Jillian's Coffee House & Bistro at 674 W Diversey Pkwy

**Days Inn Lincoln Park North** (4, D3)
This 70s-style motor inn is one of the best-value hotels in Chicago. It's clean, the staff is friendly, and it has modern conveniences like air-con that other budget hotels may lack. Otherwise, it's low on charm, but at these prices and at this location, who cares.
✉ 644 W Diversey Pkwy, Lincoln Park ☎ 773-525-7010, 888-576-3297; fax 773-525-6998 e www.daysinn .com ⊙ Diversey
🚌 22, 36 ✗ Jillian's Coffee House & Bistro at 674 W Diversey Pkwy

## Travels with Rover & Ruthie

A good number of Chicago hotels welcome visitors traveling with four-legged companions, including the **Residence Inn**, the **Claridge**, the **Red Roof** and the three Kimpton properties **Hotel Allegro**, **Hotel Burnham** and **Hotel Monaco**. Dogs are welcome at the **Radisson** if they're under 35lb. If you've left your pet at home and need someone to come home to while you're on the road, the **Hotel Monaco** will provide a goldfish for the length of your stay, free of charge.

Traveling with children is even easier than traveling with pets. The large hotels and North Side motels are kid-friendly places, with swimming pools and exercise facilities to keep kids busy, kid's portions on the menus in the coffee shops to keep kids fed and babysitters on call to give parents a break.

**Hotel Majestic** (4, B3)
A small (55-room) property on a quiet side street just off Lake Shore Dr two blocks from the shops and scenes of Wrigleyville and Lakeview. A mix of small rooms and small suites, refurbished in a warm (some say frou-frou) English style. Breakfast is included, parking is not.
✉ **528 W Brompton Ave, Wrigleyville**
☎ **773-404-3499, 1-800-727-5108; fax 773-404-3495**
e **www.cityinns.com**
🚇 Addison 🚌 151, 152
✕ **Angelina Ristorante (p. 74)**

**Howard Johnson** (5, F4) This two-story motel smack in the heart of the city offers clean rooms, a nice staff and coffee in the rooms to complement the incredible location. There's free parking but it's first-come, first-served as there are only 30 spaces for 73 guest rooms.
✉ **720 N LaSalle St, River North** ☎ **312-664-8100,**

1-800-446-4656; fax 312-664-2365
e **www.hojo.com**
🚇 Chicago (Brown)
🚌 156 ✕ **Café Luna**

**Ohio House Motel** (5, G4) There are those who claim this place is untouched since JFK was president. It certainly looks vintage, reminding one that life and motel rooms were simpler then. The 50 rooms are clean if not necessarily inspiring, the rates are rock-bottom and the location is superb.
✉ **600 N LaSalle St, River North** ☎ **312-943-3600; fax 312-943-6063** 🚇 Grand 🚌 156
✕ **Ohio House Coffee Shop**

**Red Roof** (5, G6) Formerly a Motel 6, this 191-room property was undergoing a full makeover at press time. Management insists that the prices (some of the lowest in the neighborhood) will remain low and that the friendly staff will remain in place

and presumably just as friendly. Pets allowed, discounted parking available.
✉ **162 E Ontario St, Near North**
☎ **312-787-3580; fax 312-787-1299**
🚇 Grand 🚌 3, 145, 146, 147, 151, 157
✕ **Newsmaker Café (at Best Western Inn next door)**

**The Willows** (4, D3) Another small property from the people who operate City Suites on Belmont Ave and the Majestic on Brompton Ave. This has the best location, on a quiet block steps from the convergence of Clark, Diversey and Broadway. The rooms have been redone in soothing green and pink tones, consistent with the name.
✉ **555 W Surf St, Lakeview** ☎ **773-528-8400, 1-800-787-3108; fax 773-528-8483**
e **www.cityinns.com**
🚇 Diversey 🚌 22, 36
✕ **Jillian's Coffee House & Bistro at 674 W Diversey Pkwy**

# facts for the visitor

Buckingham fountain, Grant Park

# ARRIVAL & DEPARTURE

Chicago is one of the most important air transport centers in North America, if not the world.

It has nonstop service to most major destinations in Europe and the Americas and to Tokyo and Hong Kong.

Travelers from elsewhere in Asia or Africa can make connections in London, Paris or Frankfurt and travelers from the South Pacific can make connections in San Francisco or Los Angeles.

## Air

Two major airports serve Chicago, both well connected to the city by rapid transit, commuter rail and conventional ground transport.

## O'Hare International

O'Hare International (3, B1), 17 miles northwest of downtown, has over 70 million passengers passing through a year, most of them changing planes, as in the railroad era when travelers changed trains in Chicago on their way from one coast to the other.

United Airlines has its own terminal, a glass-and-steel greenhouse recalling the old train terminals. The three other airlines share the three other domestic and international terminal buildings. There are no luggage storage facilities at O'Hare.

### Information

| | |
|---|---|
| General Inquiries | ☎ 1-800-832-6352 |
| Flight Information | |
| American | ☎ 1-800-223-5436 |
| British Airways | ☎ 1-800-247-9297 |
| Continental | ☎ 1-800-784-4444 |
| Delta | ☎ 1-800-241-4141 |
| Northwest | ☎ 1-800-225-2525 |
| United | ☎ 1-800-241-6522 |
| Car Park Information | ☎ 1-800-547-5673 |
| Hotel Booking Service | ☎ 877-456-3446 |

### Airport Access

**Train** The CTA Blue Line starts right inside the O'Hare terminal complex, but it may be a long hike to the platform which is cunningly hidden somewhere under the Hilton Hotel next to Terminal 2. Trains run 24hrs. The one-way fare is $1.50, but you can buy a visitors pass at the station.

The Airport Transit System (ATS) connects all of the terminals with long-term parking and the O'Hare station on the North Central Metra line, which runs from Union Station downtown to Antioch on the Wisconsin border. The one-way Metra fare to Union Station is $3.15, children 7-11 half-price.

Continental Airport Express runs shuttles to downtown hotels every 5-10mins. One-way fares are $17.50/8.50, adult roundtrips $31. Discounts are available for two or more passengers traveling together who buy roundtrip tickets at the airport. Buy tickets at the kiosks in the baggage claim areas.

**Taxi** There are taxi stands in front of each terminal. Full fares to the Near North Side or downtown will cost $35-40. Travelers headed to the Near North Side or downtown can share a ride with up to three others for a flat fee of $19 each. Be sure to say you want to share.

**Car** If you're driving, take the Kennedy Expressway (I-90) straight into town. Exit at Ohio St if you're headed to the Near North Side, or take one of The Loop exits if you're headed into downtown.

## Midway Airport

Midway (3, H5) is 10 miles southwest of downtown. It generally serves commuter and shorter-haul carriers such as Southwest Airlines. There are no luggage storage facilities at Midway.

## Information

General Inquiries   ☎ 773-838-0600

Flight Information

| | |
|---|---|
| American | ☎ 1-800-223-5436 |
| Continental | ☎ 1-800-784-4444 |
| Northwest | ☎ 1-800-225-2525 |
| Southwest | ☎ 435-9792 |

Car Park Information ☎ 773-838-0756

Hotel Booking Service

           ☎ 877-456-3446

### Airport Access

**Train** The CTA Orange Line runs from Midway to downtown, where it connects with other CTA El lines. The one-way fare is $1.50, but you can buy a visitors pass at the station.

Continental Airport Express runs shuttles to downtown hotels every 5-10mins. One-way fares are $12.50/8, adult roundtrip $23. Discounts are available for two or more passengers traveling together who buy roundtrip tickets at the airport. Buy tickets in the terminal opposite the Southwest counter.

**Taxi** There are taxi stands in front of each terminal. Full fare to the Near North Side or downtown will cost about $19. Travelers headed to the Near North or downtown can share a ride with up to three others for $14 each. Be sure to tell the dispatcher or the driver you want to share.

**Car** If you're driving, take Cicero Ave north from the airport to the Stevenson Expressway (I-55) and follow the signs to the Dan Ryan Expressway (I-90/ I-94) north to The Loop or the Ohio St exit if you're headed to the Near North Side.

## Train

Chicago is still the hub of US rail travel. Amtrak provides direct service to the East Coast, the West Coast, New Orleans, Texas, Toronto and various destinations in the Midwest from Union Station. Call ☎ 1-800-872-7245 or check ⓔ www.amtrak.com.

## Bus

Chicago is also a hub for bus travel. Greyhound (5, N2; ☎ 1-800-231-2222, ⓔ www.greyhound.com) provides nationwide service from its main station downtown at 630 W Harrison St and limited service from Union Station.

## Travel Documents

### Passport

Canadians need proof of Canadian citizenship or a passport to enter the US. All other visitors must have a valid passport, which should be valid for at least six months longer than their intended stay in the US.

### Visa

Travelers from countries such as Argentina, Australia, Austria, Belgium, Denmark, France, Germany, Ireland, Italy, Japan, the Netherlands, New Zealand, Spain and Switzerland can enter the US for up to 90 days under the reciprocal visa-waiver program if they have a roundtrip ticket that is nonrefundable in the US and have a passport valid for at least six months past their scheduled departure date.

For the updated list of countries included in this program, see the Immigration and Naturalization Service website, ⓔ www.ins.gov or call ☎ 1-800-375-5283. All other travelers will need a visitor's visa. Visas can be obtained at most US consulate offices overseas; however, it is generally easier to obtain a visa from an office in your home country.

### Return/Onward Ticket

Travelers under the reciprocal visa-waiver program will need return or onward tickets to enter the US. Travelers applying for visas overseas will generally require such tickets as proof of their intent to return home.

## Customs

All incoming travelers must fill out customs declarations. Travelers must specifically disclose all agricultural products and all cash and cash equivalents worth $10,000 or more.

## Duty Free

Overseas visitors may bring in up to $100 in goods or gifts duty free, together with 100 cigars, 200 cigarettes and 1L of alcoholic beverages. Cuban tobacco products are prohibited in the US.

## Departure Tax

There are no separate departure taxes to leave a US airport. Any airport charges will be included in the cost of your ticket.

# GETTING AROUND

Driving in Chicago presents the usual challenges of big-city life – tough traffic and even tougher parking. Most visitor sites are within a mile of the lakefront and you can reach almost any place you want to go by walking or taking public transport. In the lakefront districts, you'll find a major street every half-mile (four to eight blocks) with an El stop and a bus line.

## Travel Passes

The Chicago Transit Authority (CTA) sells visitor passes good for anywhere from one day ($5) to five days ($18). You can buy passes at the airports, at visitor centers, or in advance (☎ 888-968-7282 or e www.transitchicago.com). Locals usually buy seven-day passes, which go for $20 at currency exchanges around town (cash only). Passes are convenient and valuable if you are moving around a lot, as normal one-way fares for the El and bus lines are $1.50, or $1.80 with a transfer (second transfer free if used within 2hrs; free transfers permitted at some elevated and subway stations, check CTA maps).

The CTA also sells discounted transit cards ($11 value for $10, $22 value for $20) at transport stations, local supermarkets and other locations.

## Subway

The CTA subway and elevated lines, known locally as the El, run north along the lakefront to the city line and the suburbs of Evanston and Wilmette, west to the airports and the inner suburbs of Cicero, Berwyn and Oak Park, and south to the heart of the old South Side.

Some lines run underground downtown and on the Near North Side, while others run on the elevated tracks that circle downtown (the reason downtown is called 'The Loop'). The Red Line (which serves the north lakefront) and the Blue Line (which serves O'Hare) run 24-7; the other lines generally stop running some time after midnight until 5 or 6am.

Check the CTA timetables at stations or e www.transitchicago.com.

## Bus

CTA buses run on most of the major east-west and north-south streets of the city and the inner suburbs.

Most run 'til midnight, with owl service on some lines. Service is very good during peak hours morning and night, good during the day and hit-or-miss in the evenings.

Look for a sign confirming that you're at a bus stop and then hail a bus as you would a taxi. You can check timetables and route maps at CTA stations or the CTA website. PACE operates bus lines in the far west and northwestern suburbs, call ☎ 847-836-7000 or check ⓔ www.pacebus.com.

## Train

Metra operates 12 suburban rail lines from four downtown terminals, north into Wisconsin, southeast into Indiana and west into Illinois.

One-way fares run from $1.75 to $6.60 depending on the distance traveled; maps, timetables and detailed fare information are available at the terminals (Union Pacific/Northwestern, Union, LaSalle St and Randolph St stations), at ☎ 312-322-6777 or online at ⓔ www.metrarail.com.

## Taxi

Taxis are easy to come by in The Loop and the lakefront neighborhoods. You can hail a taxi on the street or queue up at taxi stands in front of some major hotels and shopping complexes. Basic charges are $1.90 flag fall, $1.60 each additional mile. Additional passengers are 50¢ apiece.

At these rates, taxis are good value for short trips, such as shopping around Near North and River North or bar-hopping along Clark or Halsted Sts. A long trip – North Side to South Side or Near North to Far North – will start to cost you.

## Car & Motorcycle

Driving in Chicago is difficult, but not impossible. If you need a car your biggest problem will be parking, which is generally available but frequently expensive. The city runs two massive garages under Grant Park (5, K7).

Enter the Grant Park North garage from the center lanes of Michigan Ave between Randolph St and Washington Blvd if you're headed south or between Madison St and Washington Blvd if heading north. Charges are $10 for the first hour going up to $19 for 24hrs.

There's an evening special, $10 if you enter after 4pm and leave before 5am. Enter the East Monroe garage at Randolph St and Columbus Dr, or Monroe St and Columbus Dr. Charges are $10 for up to 12hrs, $13 for up to 24hrs.

You'll find massive private garages elsewhere in The Loop and the Near North under or behind the Michigan Ave malls, and small parking lots in some neighborhoods, such as Lakeview. Side streets are usually reserved for neighborhood residents. If you do park improperly, you will be fined.

Fuel is easy to come by. You'll find gas stations on almost every major street in the city, except in the center of The Loop and the heart of the Near North Side.

### Road Rules

Chicagoans drive on the right. You can turn right on a red light after a full stop unless a sign says no. Don't block intersections, and don't drive a truck or van on Lake Shore Dr as it's reserved for passenger cars. Seat belts are compulsory for all front seat passengers and all passengers riding in a car if the driver is 18 or under.

The Illinois speed limit is 55mph, 30mph in urban areas and 20mph in school zones unless otherwise posted. Driving under the influence of drink or drugs is strictly prohibited. A blood alcohol level of .08% or a trace of marijuana or other controlled substances in your blood will earn a summary suspension of your license.

## Rental

You can rent a car from any of the big national car-rental chains, such as Alamo, Avis, Budget, Hertz, Enterprise, National or Thrifty, at the airports or at various city locations.

Call national toll-free directory assistance on ☎ 1-800-555-1212 for phone numbers. You will need a valid driver's license and a recognized credit card. Keep in mind that no-one rents to drivers under 21 and many companies refuse to rent to drivers under 25.

## Driving License & Permit

Canadian and Mexican driving licenses are generally accepted in the Chicago area. Other overseas travelers should carry their domestic driving licenses and an international driving permit.

## Motoring Organizations

The American Automobile Association, the pre-eminent motoring organization in the US, provides minor breakdown service, short-distance towing and other acts of mercy for its millions of members. Call ☎ 1-800-222-4357 for road service. AAA members can also get road maps at AAA offices and discounts from hotels and car rental companies. Call ☎ 1-800-922-8228, check e www.aaa.com, or go to the downtown office at 100 W Randolph St, Suite 213, ☎ 1-800-222-5347.

# PRACTICAL INFORMATION

## Climate & When to Go

Chicago sits about halfway between the Gulf of Mexico and Hudson Bay and there's not much more than a couple of hills in either direction to block the breezes from north or south. The winter is brutal, the spring changeable, the summers warm and occasionally oppressive. Fall is the most dependable season, dry and crisp and ornamented by the turning leaves.

The best times to visit are summer, when locals and visitors fill the parks and city sidewalks late into the evenings, and the fall, when Chicago gets back to business and sets out its holiday lights.

Whenever you decide to go, check the convention schedule (p. 104). Chicago is a big city, but it hosts some of the biggest meetings, conventions and shows in the world and there are times during the year when you won't be able to find a hotel room for either love nor money.

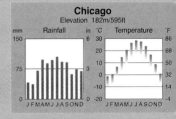

**Chicago**
Elevation 182m/595ft
Rainfall / Temperature charts (mm, in, °C, °F), months J F M A M J J A S O N D

## Tourist Information

### Tourist Information Abroad

The US has no tourist information offices overseas, so see the following Chicago-based services or log on to the websites on page 117 for information to help plan your trip.

### Local Tourist Information

The Chicago Convention and Tourism Bureau provides a wide range of tourist information, from maps and brochures about city sights to online hotel and restaurant reservations. Visit e www.chicago.il.org, call ☎ 312-567-8500 or visit the Visitor Information Centers downtown at the Chicago Cultural Center (5, K6; 77 E Randolph St), Mon-Fri 10am-6pm, Sat 10am-5pm, Sun 11am-5pm (closed holidays) or on the Near North Side at the Water Tower (5, E6; 163 E Pearson St), daily 7.30am-7pm (closed Thanksgiving and Christmas).

## Embassies & Consulates

### Australia
1601 Massachusetts Ave NW, Washington, DC 20008 (☎ 202-797-3000; after-hours emergency ☎ 888-239-3501)

### Canada
180 N Stetson Ave, Suite 2400, Chicago IL 60601 (5, J6; ☎ 312-616-1860)

### France
737 N Michigan Ave, Suite 2020, Chicago 60611 (5, F6; ☎ 312-787-5359)

### Germany
676 N Michigan Ave, Suite 3200, Chicago 60611 (5, F6; ☎ 312-580-1199)

### Ireland
400 N Michigan Ave, Suite 911, Chicago IL 60611 (5, H6; ☎ 312-337-1868)

### Mexico
300 N Michigan Ave, Suite 200, Chicago IL 60601 (5, J6; ☎ 312-855-1380)

### New Zealand
37 Observatory Circle, Washington DC 20008 (☎ 202-328-4800)

### South Africa
3051 Massachusetts Ave NW, Washington DC 20008 (☎ 202-232-4400)

### UK
400 N Michigan Ave, Suite 1300, Chicago IL 60611 (5, H6; ☎ 312-346-1810)

## Money

### Currency
US dollars are the only currency accepted in Chicago. The US dollar is divided into 100 cents (1¢). Coins come in denominations of 1¢ (a penny), 5¢ (nickels), 10¢ (dimes), 25¢ (quarters), 50¢ (half-dollars) and $1 (dollars). Although a new dollar coin has been issued, one rarely sees dollar coins or half-dollar coins. Quarters are the handiest coins, for both vending machines and parking meters. US bills are all the same color and the same size. They come in $1, $2, $5, $10, $20, $50 and $100 denominations, but $2 bills are extremely rare.

### Travelers Checks
Traveler's checks, which can be replaced if they are lost or stolen, are good as cash in the US if they are in US dollars (although some fast food joints and small restaurants may refuse to take them). Keep a record of the check numbers separate from the checks themselves.

### Credit Cards
Major credit cards are accepted just about everywhere from hotels and restaurants to shops and gas stations. You will need major credit cards for certain transactions, such as renting a car, registering for a hotel room or buying tickets to a play or sporting event.

Visa and MasterCard are the most commonly accepted, followed by American Express and Discover cards. Places that accept Visa and MasterCard usually accept corresponding sponsored debit cards. Carry copies of your credit card numbers separately from your cards. If your cards are lost or stolen, contact the company immediately. For 24hr card cancellations, call:

| | |
|---|---|
| American Express | ☎ 1-800-528-4800 |
| Diners Club | ☎ 1-800-234-6377 |
| Discover | ☎ 1-800-347-2683 |
| MasterCard | ☎ 1-800-826-2181 |
| Visa | ☎ 1-800-336-8472 |

### ATMs
ATMs are a good alternative to travelers checks, particularly for

overseas visitors who would otherwise have to stand in line somewhere to change money. ATMs are all over town – in airports and train stations, outside banks and inside liquor stores.

Almost all accept cards from the Cirrus, Star and Global Access networks. Charges to use ATMs other than your own bank's machines usually start at 50¢; most machines will disclose the amount of the charge and ask whether you want to proceed before they give you your cash.

### Changing Money

Banks usually offer better rates than exchange offices. To change foreign currency, go downtown to American National Bank & Trust at 1 N LaSalle St (5, K4; ☎ 312-661-5000) or Northern Trust Bank at 50 S LaSalle St (5, L4; ☎ 312-630-6000). American Express has a location in The Loop at 122 S Michigan Ave (5, L6; ☎ 312-435-2595) and another in Lincoln Park at 2338 N Clark St (4, E4; ☎ 773-477-4000).

There's a currency exchange in the international terminal at O'Hare airport that is usually open and overseas visitors can use ATM cards to get US cash almost anywhere, at bank rates.

## Tipping

Tipping is customary in bars, restaurants and better hotels. Tip your server at a restaurant 15% (unless the service is terrible) and 20% or more if the service is great. Tip the bartender $1 for one or two beers, or 15% if you are buying a round. Tip taxi drivers $1 on a fare of $6 or less, 10% from there on up.

Baggage carriers should get $1 a bag, and valet parkers $2 when they hand you the keys to your car.

Doormen should get $1-2 to get you a cab, the concierge at your hotel $5 or more for booking a table or theater tickets, and the maid at your hotel $1-2 a night.

## Discounts

Many museums, tours and sights have discount tickets for children and seniors. If you are going to be in Chicago for a few days, buy a CityPass at the Visitor Centers in the Chicago Cultural Center (5, K6), the Water Tower (5, E6) and Navy Pier (5, G10) or at any HotTix stand (see p. 87) to save up to 50% on standard, adult or children's admissions to six big sights in town – the Adler Planetarium, the Art Institute, the Field Museum, the Museum of Science & Industry, the Sears Tower and the Shedd Aquarium. You can buy a CityPass in advance online at ℮ www.citypass.net.

### Student & Youth Cards

The CTA does not recognize student/youth cards from out of town. Most student and teacher discounts are reserved for students and teachers from local institutions.

### Seniors' Cards

Seniors can get discounts at some sights and hotels. Ask if you don't see a sign. Some discounts apply to persons 50 and over, others to persons 60 or 65 and over. The CTA does not discount El or bus fares for seniors from out of town.

## Travel Insurance

A policy covering theft, loss, medical expenses and compensation for cancellation or delays in your travel arrangements is highly recommended. If items are lost or stolen, make sure you get a police report straight away – otherwise your insurer might not pay up.

## Opening Hours

Most offices are open 8.30am or 9am to 5pm or 5.30pm Mon-Fri.

Most shops are from about 10am to about 7pm Mon-Sat, noon to 6pm on Sunday. Restaurants are usually open daily 11.30am-2pm for lunch and about 5.30-10pm or 11pm for dinner. Most shops are open on public holidays (except for July 4th, Thanksgiving, Christmas and New Year's Day), but banks, schools, offices and some museums (call ahead) will usually be closed.

## Public Holidays

| | |
|---|---|
| Jan 1 | New Year's Day |
| 3rd Mon in Jan | Martin Luther King Jr Day |
| 3rd Mon in Feb | President's Day |
| 1st Mon in Mar | Pulaski Day |
| Mar/Apr | Easter Sunday |
| 3rd Mon in Apr | Patriot's Day |
| Last Mon in May | Memorial Day |
| Jul 4 | Independence Day |
| 1st Mon in Sept | Labor Day |
| 2nd Mon in Oct | Columbus Day |
| Nov 11 | Veterans' Day |
| 4th Thurs in Nov | Thanksgiving |
| Dec 25 | Christmas Day |

## Time

Chicago is in the Central Standard Time Zone which is 6hrs behind GMT/UTC. Daylight saving time runs from the first Sunday of April to the last Saturday of October. At noon in Chicago it's:

1pm in New York
10am in Los Angeles
6pm in London
7pm in Johannesburg
4am (following day) in Auckland
2am (following day) in Sydney

## Electricity

Electricity in the US is 110v and 60Hz. Plugs have either two or three pins (two flat, with an optional round grounding pin). Adaptors for European and South American plugs are common. Australians should bring their own adaptors.

## Weights & Measures

Americans still use what they call the English system of weights and measures. Distances come in inches, feet, yards and miles; dry weights in ounces, pounds and tons; liquid volumes in pints, quarts and gallons. The US gallon contains about 20% less than the imperial gallon because it only amounts to four quarts. See the conversion table on page 121.

## Post

The Loop station in the Chicago Federal Center at 211 S Clark St (5, L5; ☎ 312-427-4225) and the Ontario station at 227 E Ontario St (5, G7; ☎ 312-642-7698) are the most convenient post office locations for travelers. Other branches are listed in the 'Government Listings' section of the white pages of the telephone directory.

### Postal Rates

Buy stamps at post offices or at certain bank ATMs. At press time, first-class mail within the US is 34¢ for letters to one ounce (22¢ each additional ounce) and 20¢ for postcards. International airmail to locations other than Canada and Mexico is 60¢ for a half-ounce letter and 55¢ for a postcard. Letters to Canada are 46¢ for half-ounce letters and letters to Mexico are 40¢ for the first half-ounce.

### Opening Hours

The Loop station is open 7am-6pm Mon-Fri and the Ontario station is open 8am-6pm Mon-Fri. The main post office at 433 S Harrison St in the West Loop (5, N3; ☎ 312-654-3895) is open 24-7.

## Telephone

Public telephones are generally coin-operated, although some pay phones accept phonecards and some even accept credit cards. Phone booths are relatively common, despite the recent explosion in mobile phone service. The Ameritech phones (run by the local phone company) are generally reliable and cost 35¢ for a local call.

The city is divided into two different area codes. The Loop and the rest of the city center (to roughly 1600 north, south and west) is in the 312 area code. The remainder of the city is in the 773 area code. See other suburban areas below. You do not need to dial the area code to make a local call; if you dial the code when you shouldn't or don't dial the code when you should, the phone company will set you right.

## County & City Codes

| | |
|---|---|
| USA | ☎ 1 |
| The Loop & city center | ☎ 312 |
| Remainder of Chicago | ☎ 773 |
| North Suburbs | ☎ 847 |
| West & South Suburbs | ☎ 708 |
| Far West Suburbs | ☎ 630 |

## Phonecards

Prepaid phonecards are sold at newsstands and pharmacies around town, but they can be a rip-off. The MCI/Worldcom cards sold in a variety of denominations at Walgreen's are probably the best overall value. Lonely Planet's eKno Communication Card, specifically aimed at travelers, provides competitive international calls (avoid using for local calls), messaging services and free email. Log onto e www.ekno.lonelyplanet.com for information on joining and accessing the service. If you are using a credit card to make local calls, use a major carrier such as AT&T (☎ 800-321-0288) or Sprint (☎ 800-877-4646).

## Mobile Phones

The US uses a variety of mobile phone systems, only one of which is a GMS remotely compatible with systems used outside of North America. Most North American travelers can use their mobiles in the Chicago area, but they should check with their carriers about roaming charges before they start racking up the minutes.

## Useful Numbers

| | | |
|---|---|---|
| Local Directory Inquiries | ☎ | 411 |
| International Directory Inquiries | ☎ | 412-555-1515 |
| International Dialing Code | ☎ | 011 |
| International Operator | ☎ | 00 |
| Collect (reverse-charge) | ☎ | 0 |
| Operator Assisted Calls (+dial the number, an operator will come on after you have dialed) | ☎ | 01 |
| Time | ☎ | 976-1616 |
| Weather | ☎ | 976-1212 |

## International Codes

Dial 0 then:

| | |
|---|---|
| Australia | ☎ 61 |
| Canada | ☎ 1 |
| France | ☎ 33 |
| Germany | ☎ 49 |
| Japan | ☎ 81 |
| New Zealand | ☎ 64 |
| South Africa | ☎ 27 |
| UK | ☎ 44 |

# Digital Resources

You can check your emails at the public libraries, including the Harold G Washington Library in The Loop at (5, M5; 400 S State St), an internet cafe or by buying computer time at your nearest Kinko's (see p. 117).

## Internet Service Providers

America On Line is the 800-pound gorilla of ISPs in the US. The other two major ISPs are Microsoft Network and Earthlink/Mindspring. Access AOL on ☎ 312-986-5900 or ☎ 773-570-4265, MSN on ☎ 312-986-2476 or ☎ 773-442-1520, and Earthlink on ☎ 312-546-4492.

## Internet Cafes

If you can't access the Internet from where you're staying, head to Screenz (4, D3; 2717 N Clark St; ☎ 773-388-8300), the only real cybercafe in town and a sleek spot with upholstered booths, French espresso and T-1 lines; open Mon-Thurs 8am-midnight, Fri 8am-1am, Sat 9am-1am, Sun 9am-midnight. Access is 6¢/min ($1 minimum).

## Useful Sites

Lonely Planet's website (e www .lonelyplanet.com) offers a speedy link to many of Chicago's websites. Others to try include:

Official City of Chicago Site
  e www.ci.chi.il.us

Chicago Metromix
  e www.metromix.com

Chicago Reader
  e www.chicagoreader.com

Chicago Tribune
  e www.chicagotribune.com

Chicago CitySearch
  e www.chicago.citysearch.com

## CitySync

CitySync *Chicago*, Lonely Planet's digital guide for Palm OS hand-held devices, allows quick search-es, sorting and bookmarking of hundreds of Chicago's attractions, clubs, hotels, restaurants and more – all pinpointed on scrollable street maps. Purchase or demo CitySync *Chicago* at e www.city sync.com.

## Doing Business

Kinko's stores in The Loop (5, J5; 6 W Lake St; ☎ 312-424-6700) and Lakeview (3, C3; 3001 N Clark St; ☎ 773-528-0500) have worksta-tions, fax machines, copiers and Internet access 24-7. Other Kinko's locations have the same facilities but close at varying times in the evening.

Most large hotels and some smaller ones have business centers where you can find workstations, fax machines, copiers and Internet access.

Business travelers looking for information about doing business in the area should contact the Chicagoland Chamber of Com-merce (330 N Wabash Ave; ☎ 312-494-6700, e www.chicagoland chamber.org).

## Newspapers & Magazines

Chicago has two daily newspapers – *The Chicago Tribune*, which still calls itself 'The World's Greatest Newspaper,' and the *Chicago Sun-Times*, a tabloid now owned by Canadian newspaper magnate Conrad Black. The *Tribune* used to be known for its quirky spelling and its extreme right-wing views. Today it is an even-handed quality paper with outstanding arts and culture coverage. The *Sun-Times* has good local coverage and a stable of great columnists. Many Chicagoans read the *Sun-Times* for local news and the national edition of *The New York Times* for everything else.

*Chicago Magazine* is a glossy monthly catering to the profession-al classes, filled with restaurant reviews and cultural news. The *Reader* is a free weekly with excep-tional entertainment coverage. If you want your news in Spanish, Korean or Polish, try one of the dozens of local weeklies on the newsstands that cater to the city's immigrant communities.

## Radio

Chicago has one of the best public radio stations in the country, WBEZ (91.5FM), home of *This American Life* and other NPR programs. For conventional news radio, try WBBM (780AM). The best rock sta-tion in town is WXRT (93.1FM). If light rock is your thing, try its neighbor WLIT (93.9FM).

Other stations worth trying include WSCR (sports talk, 670AM), WFMT (classical, 98.7FM), WOJO (Spanish, 105.1FM) and WGCI (urban contemporary, 107.5FM).

## TV

You'll find the usual US suspects on the small screen. WGN-TV (Channel 9), the Tribune TV outlet, broadcasts the Cubs games and WTTW (Channel 11), the PBS affiliate, has an in-depth look at one of the day's big stories every weekday at 7pm. Spanish-speaking travelers can tune in to WSNS (Channel 44) for the latest news or telenovela.

## Photography & Video

For equipment and film, head to Central Camera (232 S Wabash Ave; ☎ 312-427-5580) for an extraordinary selection, or Best Buy (1000 W North Ave; ☎ 312-988-4067) for a great selection at great prices. Overseas visitors shopping for videos should remember that the US uses the NTSC system, which is incompatible with the PAL (UK and Australasia) and SECAM formats (most of Western Europe).

## Health

### Immunizations

No vaccinations or immunizations are required to enter the US.

### Precautions

You can drink the water in Chicago (although many residents prefer the bottled stuff) and you can breathe the air. If you do exercise or spend a lot of time in the sun, drink plenty of fluids and take breaks.

Like anywhere else, the usual precautions apply when it comes to sex. Condoms are available at any pharmacy and most corner stores.

## Insurance & Medical Treatment

Overseas visitors should have medical insurance before they come to Chicago, as medical care can be very expensive in the US and many doctors and hospitals insist on payment before treatment.

### Medical Services

The Northwestern Memorial Hospital (5, F7; 225 E Huron St; ☎ 312-926-2000) is a terrific institution, and the most convenient location to the Near North and Gold Coast. In an emergency, dial ☎ 911 for an ambulance. Remember that ER charges are extremely expensive. Other hospitals include:

Illinois Masonic
  (4, C3; ☎ 773-975-1600) 836 W Wellington

University of Chicago Hospital
  (7, E3; ☎ 773-702-1000) 5841 S Maryland Ave

Children's Memorial Hospital
  (4, E3; ☎ 773-880-4000) 2300 N Lincoln Ave

### Dental Services

Dental service is available at the University of Illinois Dental School (3, E7, 801 S Paulina St, ☎ 312-996-7555) Mon-Fri from 8am to 4pm (patients are requested to register by 2pm). The Chicago Dental Society hotline at ☎ 630-978-5745 will provide referrals any time including nights and weekends.

### Pharmacies

The Near North Walgreen's (5, F6; 757 N Michigan Ave; ☎ 312-664-8586) and the Lakeview Osco (4, C3; 3101 N Clark St; ☎ 773-477-1967) are open 24-7. Both have branches all over town, some also open 24-7. Call Osco on ☎ 888-443-5701 or Walgreen's on ☎ 1-800-925-4733.

## Toilets

Public toilets are few and far between and most small restaurants and coffee shops restrict their restrooms to customers. The Visitor Centers at the Chicago Cultural Center and the Water Tower are generally open 10am to 7pm Mon-Sat, noon to 5pm Sun. The large hotels, shopping malls and public buildings usually have facilities that are clean and easy to find.

## Safety Concerns

It's a big city out there, so use some common sense. Don't carry around huge amounts of cash, and lock up what you don't need if your hotel has a safe or safety deposit boxes. Don't carry your wallet in your backpack or your back pocket. Stay out of dim, empty streets after dark.

Unless you're traveling with locals, it's probably a good idea to stay east of Halsted St on the West Side (take a taxi or a bus to the United Center, Little Italy or Cook County Hospital) and inside the confines of Hyde Park-Kenwood on the South Side (Cottage Grove Ave east to the lake). The lines between safe and unsafe areas are a little more irregular on the North and Northwest Sides, but keep your eyes open as neighborhoods can change dramatically in a couple of blocks.

Some El platforms have special nighttime waiting areas. Use them.

### Lost Property

For the CTA system, call customer service on ☎ 888-968-6282. For Metra call: Union Station (☎ 312-322-4269), Union Pacific Station (☎ 312-496-4777), LaSalle St Station (☎ 312-322-8957), Randolph St Station (☎ 312-322-7819).

### Keeping Copies

Make photocopies of all your important documents, keep some with you, separate from the originals, and leave a copy at home. You can also store details of documents in Lonely Planet's free online Travel Vault, password-protected and accessible worldwide. See |e| www .ekno.lonelyplanet.com.

## Emergency Numbers

Police, fire,
  ambulance      ☎ 911
Police Information ☎ 312-746-6000
Rape Crisis Line   ☎ 312-744-8418

## Women Travelers

Women are as safe in Chicago as they are in any big American city. The usual precautions apply about paying attention to your surroundings and taking a little extra care walking at night. Women may encounter obnoxious behavior after dark, particularly on the weekends, but most men will probably let it go if you just ignore them and keep on moving.

Tampons and pads are widely available, though there's a smaller selection of tampons than in Europe and Australia. The contraceptive pill is available by prescription only and the 'morning after' pill is technically available by prescription but harder to come by.

## Gay & Lesbian Travelers

Illinois was the first state in the US to decriminalize consensual sexual acts between adults, but no-one would mistake Chicago for Key West or Mykonos (Midwesterners are a bit reserved whatever their orientation).

That said, the local community is numerous and visible, particularly on the North Side where the area from Belmont to Irving Park Rd is sometimes called Boystown. This is the one area in town where you'll see open displays of public affection. Lesbian life is centered a little farther north up Clark St, in Andersonville.

## Information & Organizations

Chicago has two gay weeklies – the established *Windy City Times* and the new *Chicago Free Press*. Both are available free on newsstands on the North Side and elsewhere around town.

The Chicago Area Gay & Lesbian Chamber of Commerce (3713 N Halsted St; ☎ 773-871-4190; [e]www.glchamber.org) is open 11am-6pm Mon-Sat, 11am-3pm Sun.

Horizons (961 W Montana St; ☎ 773-472-6469) is a social service agency for the community that also provides a safe space for gay youth to relax. Its LGBT hotline (☎ 773-929-4357) has taped messages about community events.

For HIV-related questions, call the Aids Foundation of Chicago (411 S Wells St, Suite 300; ☎ 1-800-243-2437 or ☎ 312-922-2322). For other health questions, try the Chicago Women's Health Center (3435 N Sheffield Ave; ☎ 773-935-6126) noon to 4pm Mon-Fri, or the Howard Brown Health Center (945 W George St; ☎ 773-388-1600), the Midwest's largest lesbian, gay and bisexual health organization.

## Senior Travelers

Chicago is a great destination for seniors. The public transit network and flat sidewalks make the city easy to navigate, and there is a wide range of things to do, from museums to parks to nightspots. If your bones are brittle or your step is unsure, avoid the winter months when snow, ice and wind can make it hard to cross the street.

### Information & Organizations

The American Association of Retired Persons (AARP; ☎ 1-800-424-3410; [e] www.aarp.org; 601 E St NW, Washington, DC 20049), a lobbying group for Americans 50 years and older, has hotel and car rental discounts for members.

## Disabled Travelers

Chicago is not a particularly good city for the mobility impaired. True, it is flat and most of the sidewalks have curb cuts, but many of the buildings are old, with stairs and narrow entries, and most of the public transit system is unequipped to handle wheelchairs. Some of the El stations do have elevators, as do half or more of the CTA buses.

The Metra system is supposed to be completely wheelchair accessible, but you're well advised to check with the station before you leave to smoke out any problems you might have boarding or leaving your train. Look for the ♿ listed with individual reviews

### Information & Organizations

The Mayor's Office for People with Disabilities (☎ 312-744-6673, TTY 312-744-7833) is a good place to start looking for information about services for disabled travelers. Mobility International USA (☎ 541-343-1284; fax 541-343-6812; PO Box 10767, Eugene, OR 97440) advises disabled travelers on mobility issues and runs education programs.

The Society for Accessible Travel & Hospitality (☎ 212-447-7284, [e] www.sath.org; 347 5th Ave, Suite 610, New York, NY 10016) publishes *Open World*, a magazine for disabled travelers.

## Language

Chicagoans speak English, with a variant of a Midwestern accent that is generally understandable by other English speakers.

You might hear some 'dees, dems and dos' reminiscent of the first Mayor Daley coming out of the mouths of local Irish or Slavic residents, and you will certainly hear a lot of Mississippi Delta sounds from the mouths of local African-Americans. Don't be surprised if you hear plenty of other languages.

## Conversion Table

### Clothing Sizes
*Measurements approximate only; try before you buy.*

**Women's Clothing**

| Aust/NZ | 8 | 10 | 12 | 14 | 16 | 18 |
|---|---|---|---|---|---|---|
| Europe | 36 | 38 | 40 | 42 | 44 | 46 |
| Japan | 5 | 7 | 9 | 11 | 13 | 15 |
| UK | 8 | 10 | 12 | 14 | 16 | 18 |
| USA | 6 | 8 | 10 | 12 | 14 | 16 |

**Women's Shoes**

| Aust/NZ | 5 | 6 | 7 | 8 | 9 | 10 |
|---|---|---|---|---|---|---|
| Europe | 35 | 36 | 37 | 38 | 39 | 40 |
| France only | 35 | 36 | 38 | 39 | 40 | 42 |
| Japan | 22 | 23 | 24 | 25 | 26 | 27 |
| UK | 3½ | 4½ | 5½ | 6½ | 7½ | 8½ |
| USA | 5 | 6 | 7 | 8 | 9 | 10 |

**Men's Clothing**

| Aust/NZ | 92 | 96 | 100 | 104 | 108 | 112 |
|---|---|---|---|---|---|---|
| Europe | 46 | 48 | 50 | 52 | 54 | 56 |
| Japan | S | | M | M | | L |
| UK | 35 | 36 | 37 | 38 | 39 | 40 |
| USA | 35 | 36 | 37 | 38 | 39 | 40 |

**Men's Shirts (Collar Sizes)**

| Aust/NZ | 38 | 39 | 40 | 41 | 42 | 43 |
|---|---|---|---|---|---|---|
| Europe | 38 | 39 | 40 | 41 | 42 | 43 |
| Japan | 38 | 39 | 40 | 41 | 42 | 43 |
| UK | 15 | 15½ | 16 | 16½ | 17 | 17½ |
| USA | 15 | 15½ | 16 | 16½ | 17 | 17½ |

**Men's Shoes**

| Aust/NZ | 7 | 8 | 9 | 10 | 11 | 12 |
|---|---|---|---|---|---|---|
| Europe | 41 | 42 | 43 | 44½ | 46 | 47 |
| Japan | 26 | 27 | 27.5 | 28 | 29 | 30 |
| UK | 7 | 8 | 9 | 10 | 11 | 12 |
| USA | 7½ | 8½ | 9½ | 10½ | 11½ | 12½ |

## Weights & Measures

### Length & Distance
1 inch = 2.54cm
1cm = 0.39 inches
1m = 3.3ft = 1.1yds
1ft = 0.3m
1km = 0.62 miles
1 mile = 1.6km
1 acre = 0.4ha

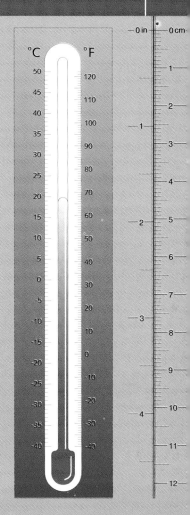

**Weight**
1kg = 2.2lb
1lb = 0.45kg
1g = 0.04oz
1oz = 28g

**Volume**
1 litre = 0.26 US gallons
1 US gallon = 3.8 litres
1 litre = 0.22 imperial gallons
1 imperial gallon = 4.55 litres

# THE AUTHOR

**Tom Given**

Tom Given was born in Chicago, where his grandmother's kitchen window looked into the left field stands at Wrigley Field. He went back to Chicago, braving ice, snow and hat-hair, to visit haunts from the past and hot spots from the present to bring you a picture of the city informed by love and a weakness for hot dogs and barbeque.

Thanks to my father Ken Given, Lakeview High '37, who taught me to see and taught me to write. Thanks, too, to Stewart Abelson, Tom Bianchi, Melinda Guttman, Fruman Jacobson, Paul Jones, Bob Kleinschmidt, David Kohn, Don Horwitz, Linda Horwitz, Phil Swarek and Patty Unterman.

# ABOUT THIS BOOK

• Design by James Hardy • Maps by Charles Rawlings-Way • Edited by Anne Mulvaney, Darren O'Connell, Gabrielle Green and Melanie Dankel • Cover by Daniel New • Publishing Manager Diana Saad • Thanks to Annie Horner, Bibiana Jaramillo, Gerard Walker, Jane Hart, Jenny Blake, Kerrie Williams, Lachlan Ross, Michele Posner, Ruth Askevold and Valerie Sinzdak.

# OTHER CONDENSED GUIDES

Other Lonely Planet Condensed guides include: *Amsterdam, Boston, California, Crete, Frankfurt, Hong Kong, London, New York City, Paris, Rome* and *Sydney*.

# ABOUT LONELY PLANET

The story begins with a classic travel adventure: Tony and Maureen Wheeler's 1972 journey across Europe and Asia to Australia. Useful information about the overland trail did not exist at that time, so Tony and Maureen published the first Lonely Planet guidebook to meet a growing need.

From a kitchen table, then from a tiny office in Melbourne, Australia, Lonely Planet has become the largest independent travel publisher in the world, an international company with offices in Melbourne, Oakland, London and Paris.

Today there are over 400 titles, including travel guides, city maps, cycling guides, first time travel guides, healthy travel guides, travel atlases, diving guides, pictorial books, phrasebooks, restaurant guides, travel literature, walking guides, watching wildlife and world food guides.

At Lonely Planet we believe that travelers can make a positive contribution to the countries they visit – if they respect their host communities and spend their money wisely. Since 1986 a percentage of the income from books has been donated to aid and human rights projects.

# LONELY PLANET ONLINE

**www.lonelyplanet.com or AOL keyword: lp**
Lonely Planet's award-winning Web site has insider info on hundreds of destinations from Amsterdam to Zimbabwe, complete with interactive maps and color photographs. You'll also find the latest travel news, recent reports from travelers on the road, guidebook upgrades and a lively bulletin board where you can meet fellow travelers, swap recommendations and seek advice.

# PLANET TALK

Our FREE quarterly printed newsletter is full of tips from travelers and anecdotes from Lonely Planet authors. Every issue is packed with up-to-date travel news and advice, and includes a postcard from Lonely Planet co-founder Tony Wheeler, mail from travelers, a look at life on the road through the eyes of a Lonely Planet author, topical health advice, prizes for the best travel yarn, news about forthcoming Lonely Planet events and a complete list of Lonely Planet books and products.

**To join our mailing list, email us at: go@lonelyplanet.co.uk (UK, Europe and Africa residents); info@lonelyplanet.com (North and South America residents); talk2us@lonelyplanet.com.au (the rest of the world); or contact any Lonely Planet office.**

# COMET

Our FREE monthly email newsletter brings you all the latest travel news, features, interviews, competitions, destination ideas, travelers' tips & tales, Q&As, raging debates and related links. Find out what's new on the Lonely Planet Web site and which books are about to hit the shelves.

**Subscribe from your desktop: www.lonelyplanet.com/comet**

## LONELY PLANET OFFICES

**Australia**
90 Maribyrnong St, Footscray, Vic 3011
☎ 613 8379 8000 fax 613 8379 8111
email: talk2us@lonelyplanet.com.au

**USA**
150 Linden St, Oakland, CA 94607
☎ 510 893 8555 TOLL FREE: 800 275 8555
fax 510 893 8572
email: info@lonelyplanet.com

**UK**
10a Spring Place, London NW5 3BH
☎ 020 7428 4800 fax 020 7428 4828
email: go@lonelyplanet.co.uk

**France**
1 rue du Dahomey, 75011 Paris
☎ 01 55 25 33 00 fax 01 55 25 33 01
email: bip@lonelyplanet.fr
minitel: 3615 lonelyplanet

**World Wide Web: www.lonelyplanet.com or AOL keyword: lp
Lonely Planet Images: lpi@lonelyplanet.com.au**

# index

*See also separate indexes for Places to Eat (p. 126), Places to Stay (p. 127), Shops (p. 127) and Sights with map references (p. 128).*

# PLACES TO EAT